PREFACE.

———◆———

THE favour which the public has accorded, and still accords, to our previous works, has induced us to offer yet another, in the hope that it may meet with the same flattering recognition enjoyed by its predecessors.

Its appearance is due not to the fact that Letter Writers are lacking in the field of useful literature—on the contrary, their name is legion—but because it is felt that the public have a right to expect a Letter Writer up to the present date, practical, sensible, and concise, written in a style suitable for everyday correspondence, and not in the stilted, and verbose language, common to the Letter Writer of thirty years ago ; in which the mass of Letter Writers at present existing would appear to be written.

The present Letter Writer is not intended to teach a

flowery and ornamental style of letter writing, but to be a
reliable guide to inexperienced letter writers in the
construction of every description of letter under every
possible circumstance.

With this aim in view, we venture to place this work in
the hands of our friends the public, and await their verdict
with pleasurable expectation.

THE CORRECT GUIDE

TO

LETTER WRITING.

BY

A MEMBER OF THE ARISTOCRACY,

AUTHOR OF "MANNERS AND RULES OF GOOD SOCIETY,"
"SOCIETY SMALL TALK," ETC., ETC.

1889.

Col. 543
ANO
MAY 13

REMARKS.

In the following Letters, to serve as forms, names have been introduced with the idea of giving them a distinct air of reality, conducive to their being better understood. Facts have also been supplied to show how personal ones may be made use of, treated, commenced, and dismissed, as facts although supposed to be easy enough to deal with in a letter, yet demand judicious handling.

Certain abbreviations are in general use in letter writing, such as the following—

c^{ld}, could ; w^{ld}, would ;
sh^{ld}, should ; &, and ;
compts., compliments ; affec^{tly}, affectionately ;
affec^{ate}, affectionate ; yrs., yours ;
v., very ; rec^{ced}, received ;
L^{d}, Lord ; advt., advertisement.
1/6/83, 1st day, 6th month, year 1883 (abbreviation
    of date used in business).

A French word is occasionally found of service, when it conveys an idea more clearly than an English word would do, or when it obviates the necessity of writing a long paragraph on the subject; but it is an affectation to make use of a French word when an English one would serve the purpose equally well.

CONTENTS.

—◆—

CHAPTER I.

CHAPTER II.

LETTERS RELATING TO ASKING FAVOURS AND MAKING REQUESTS.

CHAPTER III.

APPLYING FOR SITUATIONS. ASKING FOR AND GIVING CHARACTERS.

CHAPTER IV.

LETTERS RELATIVE TO ILLNESS AND DEATH. ANNOUNCEMENTS
AND CONDOLENCE.

CHAPTER V.

OFFERING PRESENTS. THANKING FOR PRESENTS, &c.

CHAPTER VI.

PROPOSALS OF MARRIAGE.

CHAPTER VII.

ANSWERS TO PROPOSALS OF MARRIAGE.

CHAPTER VIII.

CHAPTER IX.

FAMILY LETTERS.

CHAPTER X.

CHILDREN'S LETTERS.

CHAPTER XI.

SERVANTS' LETTERS.

CHAPTER XII.

NOTES AND LETTERS OF INVITATIONS, ANSWERS, AND POSTPONEMENTS.

CHAPTER XIII.

BUSINESS LETTERS.

CHAPTER XIV.

THE RECEIVED FORMS FOR COMMENCING, CONCLUDING, AND ADDRESSING LETTERS.

THE SOVEREIGN.

TO MEMBERS OF THE ARISTOCRACY.

THE GOVERNMENT.

CHAPTER XV.

FORMS RELATING TO BUSINESS TRANSACTIONS.

THE CORRECT GUIDE TO LETTER WRITING.

CHAPTER I.

REMARKS ON LETTER-WRITING.

THE act of writing a letter is to many people a task of
some little difficulty from various points of view. They
are at a loss as to the most fitting manner in which to
express that which they have to communicate, and one,
two, and three sheets of note paper often bear witness to
their attempts and failures. At some little point in a
letter, either at the commencement or at the finish, it
strikes them that something is not as it should be, or they
come to a dead lock altogether. Others, again, have not
the intelligence to discover for themselves that their letter
is not up to the regulation standard of notes in general,
and in consequence it is open to being considered an odd
sort of letter. In writing letters it is curious to observe
how closely any particular set of words and expressions are
followed by the generality of people, they accept a model
and adhere to it; but phrases in force in letter-writing
change, as everything else changes, and what was strictly
polite and proper to write under given circumstances some
twenty or thirty years ago, is not quite the thing to say
to-day. Thus, certain phrases arrive at a point when they
may be considered stilted, pedantic, and ponderous, or
common, and even vulgar. To commence a letter to a
comparative stranger, or to a person with whom the writer is
but slightly acquainted, on any matter of interest, is the
first difficulty to be got over. Shall it be a letter or a note,
written in the first or in the third person? This is to

B

many a perplexing question, and yet there need be no doubt on the matter, as there is a safe rule for everyone's guidance respecting it. In all communications with strangers, it would be correct to write in the third person. A very slight acquaintance, however, or a faint personal knowledge, would authorise a letter being written in the first person if it were to be of any length.

It is an accomplishment to write a good letter, and one of which few can boast, while to write a bad one is so general a practice that the receipt of a good letter almost amounts to an agreeable surprise. With regard to the composition of a letter, it should always be remembered that if it has a purpose, a reason, or an object for being written, this fact should not be lost sight of or over-weighted with a mass of extraneous matter. It is also idle to devote the first page of a letter to trivial excuses for not having written sooner, when a still longer delay might have been allowed to elapse if it suited the convenience of the writer, but when a letter requires an immediate answer, it is then a matter of politeness to give the reason for the delay, but this should be explained without circumlocution. There is not a little excuse for short-comings in the matter of letter-writing on the part of very young people; home letters have probably been their only experience in this branch of study and, with facts and affection for a basis, the compositions have not offered much difficulty during school days. It is when girls are merging into womanhood and boys into manhood, that want of fluency in letter-writing is acutely felt by them not only in youth but in after years. Some are more conscious than others of their deficiencies in this respect, and to write a letter or even a simple note, is to them a trouble and a bore; later on they take refuge in the fact that they are bad correspondents, and in saying this, it serves as an excuse for writing very short letters or for not writing at all. Many people confess when obliged to write letters, that they have no idea what to say beyond the preliminary phrase, they are afraid to trust their pen with their thoughts, for fear of getting out of their depth and of not being able to recover themselves without becoming slightly involved, and hazy as to grammar. Others have no thoughts to express beyond a vague notion that a letter has to be written and must be got through somehow. A well-expressed letter creates a pleasant feeling of gratification; it is often read twice, and

if not put by amongst other letters that are considered
worth keeping, it is destroyed almost with reluctance and
regret. One charm of a good letter lies, perhaps, in making
it personally considerate; another, that it should clearly call
to mind the individuality of the writer.

Inquiries after health in a letter should be made with
delicacy and discretion, always remembering that some are
thin-skinned on this subject, while others like to discuss it
con amore. A clever writer keeps his affairs very much in
the background unless they are at a crisis, when they would
of course possess interest of an unusual character: otherwise to relate trivial matters for the sake of having something to say is foolish and egotistical. In these days
people do not accuse themselves of writing stupid, dull, or
uninteresting letters, as their friends are only too likely to
take their compositions at their own valuation and to
endorse the written verdict; while the affectation of
laying the blame of bad writing on pens, ink, and paper is
now confined to the servants' hall, where writing materials
are perhaps not always of the best quality even when ready
to hand. In answering a letter it is a proof of a poor
imagination to minutely paraphrase each paragraph of the
letter under treatment. Questions naturally demand
answers, and important facts call for comment; but trivial
remarks and observations, perhaps pleasantly put, should
not be returned to their author with poor platitudes
attached to them. Letter writing may be said to be
divided into notes and letters. Formerly a note written in
the third person invariably commenced with, "Mrs. Jones
presents her compliments to Mrs. Brown;" but now the
words " presents compliments," have fallen very much into
disfavour; and, whenever any other opening phrase can be
readily substituted, it is in better taste to employ it.
Indeed, it may be taken as a rule that compliments are
only presented to a complete stranger, or officially, or
professionally speaking; and whenever an acquaintance-
ship exists, even of the slightest possible character, other
expressions are used in preference to the words " presents
her compliments." The nature of the note itself would
probably determine the most appropriate expression where-
with to commence it. To frame a note without introducing compliments at its commencement is the received
mode of writing one. The subject under discussion does
not require this preliminary introduction, and it is best to

embody it in the opening sentence. There are few people
careless or ignorant enough to lapse from the third person
into the first in the course of a short note; but still it is
worth guarding against. Notes are principally confined to
the briefest of communications, as the frequent and necessary repetition of the pronouns—she and her for instance
—or the surnames of the writer and recipient of the note
becomes tedious; and when it is imperative to write in the
third person, it is most desirable to construct each sentence
with a due regard to an extravagant use of pronouns, and
never at any time to resort to the vulgar expedient of
attempting a sort of compromise by making the initial
letter of the writer and of the person written to do duty
for their respective surnames.

It is observable that a cramped style, or a small Italian
handwriting, is no longer in vogue, and, when seen,
appears very much out of date. The prevailing style of
writing is bold and free. A free use of capitals is also
indulged in, which gives a dash of originality and spirit to
a letter when not over done. It used to be an idea that to
underline words in a letter was rather bad style than not;
but now, if a writer wishes to be very emphatic, or to call
particular attention to any remark, an additional stroke of
the pen is not objected to; but it is a liberty not to be
taken when writing to those with whom one is on ceremony.
Many people experience a certain difficulty in the choice of
a conventional term with which to conclude a ceremonious
letter, and it must be admitted that there is not much
variety at command, "Yours truly," "Yours sincerely,"
"Yours faithfully," with the addition perhaps of the adverb
" very," being the principal formulas in use; and it is on
the whole immaterial whether "truly" or "sincerely"
is employed when writing to friends. The affectionate
expressions addressed to still dearer friends and relations
are beside the question, and yet many devoted husbands make
use of the words " Yours truly," when writing to their
wives, in preference to any more endearing phrase. By
way of not concluding a letter too abruptly, it is usual,
before the words "Yours truly," to add one or other of such
phrases as these: "Believe me, dear Mrs. Jones," or " I
remain, dear Mrs. Jones," or " Believe me, dear Mrs. Jones,
with kind regards," and this gives a certain finish and
completeness to a letter which would otherwise be wanting.

A want of punctuation in a letter will often cause a sentence or paragraph to be misunderstood, and made to convey the reverse of what was intended. Notes of interrogation should not be omitted from a letter when questions are asked, though many consider it a waste of time to make use of them, and notes of exclamation, when required, materially assist the clearer understanding of a passage, which without them might have a vague meaning.

Another practice of the past, now happily discarded, is that of crossing letters ; only a school girl would cross and recross a sheet of writing paper, and two sheets of paper are used if one sheet will not contain all that is to be said. If half the second sheet of paper is left blank it is not torn off, a whole sheet being more convenient to hold and to fold than is half a sheet of paper, and if a few last words are necessary for the completion of a letter they are written on the margin and not across the writing on the face of the pages.

A strictly business habit is to write on the first and third pages of a sheet of note paper, leaving the second and fourth pages blank, or to write on the first and fourth pages leaving the other two unwritten upon. This is done for the convenience of having the letters so written copied by letter press. A postscript was formerly supposed to convey the pith or gist of a lady's letter—a poor compliment, it must be confessed, to her intelligence ; it is now considered a vulgarism to put P.S. at the bottom of a letter containing the few last words; if something is remembered when the letter is concluded that should have been said, it is added without apology.

In addressing envelopes the address should be written legibly in the centre of the envelope, and not run off into the corner, leaving a third of the envelope blank. Many people write their initials or name in full in one corner of the envelope ; but this is quite a matter of inclination.

CHAPTER II.

From a Lady asking for a Letter of Introduction.

December 28th, 18—.

DEAR MRS. VINCENT,

I wonder if you would mind giving me an introduction to Mrs. Percy Bathurst; I believe she is a great friend of yours, and I should much like to know her. She gives charming musical parties, and has a large acquaintance amongst the Italian residents here. I should think it very kind indeed if you would ask her to call on me. Rome is not at all full, and very few English appear to have arrived at present. We came here from Florence last Monday, and intend remaining until after Easter.

With kind regards to yourself and Mr. Vincent, believe me,

Very sincerely yours,
M. E. CONWAY.

From a Lady asking for Letters of Introduction.

LEIGH HOUSE, CHICHESTER,
November 7th, 18—.

MY DEAR MRS. EVERETT,

We propose starting for Florence next week, where we intend passing the winter. I think you told me you knew a great many residents there, and I should be most grateful for one or two letters of introduction to any of the Italian or English families, as it would make our stay so much more agreeable if we knew a few of the residents in the place. Are you thinking of going to the south of France this winter? or do you feel strong enough to encounter the English climate? I expect we shall find it

perhaps you would be able to look in at the luncheon. We
should be much pleased to see you.
With our united kind regards, believe me,
Very truly yours,
CATHERINE WILLIS.

From a Gentleman consenting to be Godfather.

6, DUNDEE PLACE, S.W.
March 2nd, 18—.

DEAR MRS. WILLIS,
I shall be happy to act as godfather to your little
boy since you and your husband are kind enough to wish it,
and I hope he will grow up to be as good a fellow as his
father. You must not expect me at the church, but I will
try and look in in the afternoon.
With kind regards to you both,
Very truly yours,
JAMES ROSS.

To a Lady asking her to be Godmother.

10, ENFIELD GARDENS, W.
June 9th, 18—.

MY DEAR MRS. ROBINSON,
I very much wish you would be godmother to my
little girl, we have named her after you, Ethel Gertrude.
She is a sweet little thing, and I shall be so proud to show
her to you. My sister Mrs. Ellis, is also to be godmother,
and my husband's brother will I hope be godfather. I
will let you know what day the christening will take place
as soon as it is decided.
With kindest remembrances from my husband and
myself, believe me,
Very sincerely yours,
BEATRICE MORRIS.

From a Lady excusing herself from being Godmother.

17, ATHOL PLACE, W.
June 10th, 18—.

DEAR MRS. MORRIS,
I must ask you to excuse me from undertaking the
office of godmother to your little daughter. The truth is,

I do not feel justified in incurring what I consider to be a great responsibility. I have always thought that the parents and near relatives of a child are most fitted for the post of sponsors, as from their position towards it, they have a better opportunity of fulfilling the promises made in its name, than those less near to it could possibly have. Other people no doubt, think differently, but these are my views, and you will not I am sure be offended at my thus frankly expressing them. I shall hope to come and see you soon, and your little Gertrude.

Believe me,

Very sincerely yours,

E. G. ROBINSON.

From a Lady to her Bankers.

5, CLIFTON GARDENS, S.W.

May 1st, 18—.

MESSRS. NORTON.

GENTLEMEN,

Will you kindly place the enclosed cheque of £200 from Messrs. Fielding, to my account, and I shall be obliged if you will forward me a cheque book of fifty cheques.

I am, Gentlemen,

Very truly yours,

MARIA HARPER.

From a Gentleman to his Bankers.

MOUNT PLEASANT VILLA, CHARLTON,

June 5th, 18—.

MESSRS. ROSKEL.

GENTLEMEN,

I am obliged by your letter of the 4th instant. I was not aware I had overdrawn my account, but I will at once attend to it, and request my solicitors, Messrs. King, to pay in a sum of £150 on Thursday next the 7th instant.

Apologising for this oversight on my part, I am, gentlemen.

Faithfully yours,

HORACE BREWSTER.

From a Lady purposing to get up a Bazaar.

ASHMEAD, TUNBRIDGE WELLS.

MRS. BARRETT presents her compliments to the Countess of Carlow and is very desirous of obtaining her patronage for a bazaar to be held in the Town-hall in June next for the benefit of the Local Hospital. Several ladies in the immediate neighbourhood have kindly promised their assistance; amongst others, Lady Sarah Linton, the Hon. Misses Carden, Mrs. Rivers, and Mrs. Churchill, and if Lady Carlow would interest herself in the undertaking either by holding a stall or by contributing articles to the bazaar, it would be of considerable service to the charity.

February 20th, 18—.

From a Gentleman soliciting a Nobleman to open a Bazaar.

DOWN GRANGE, CANTERBURY,
January 17th, 18—.

MY LORD,

May I solicit the honour of your Lordship's presence at a bazaar to be held for the benefit of the Cottage Hospital Fund at our Town-hall on the 23rd July. The ladies of the neighbourhood have taken the greatest interest in promoting this bazaar, and they are very desirous that it should be opened by your Lordship. I therefore venture to make this request, as your support and countenance would I feel sure prove of great service to the undertaking.

I beg to remain my Lord,
Yours faithfully,
ALFRED ARMSTRONG.

To the EARL OF BICESTER.

To a Lady asking her to become a Patroness.

OLDFIELD GRANGE.

MR. GRAY begs to ask the Countess of Dulwich if she will kindly allow her name to be placed on the list of lady patronesses of the Oldfield Hospital Ball to be held at the Town-hall on the 10th of next month. The Ball com-

mittee are very desirous of securing an influential list of
patronesses, as this point materially influences the sale of
tickets. Mr. Gray therefore trusts that he may count
upon the support of the Countess of Dulwich on this
occasion.

> *To the* COUNTESS OF DULWICH.
> *November 14th,* 18—.

From a Lady to a Nobleman, soliciting his Votes.

> 5, GLOUCESTER GARDENS, S.W.,
> *March 14th,* 18—.

DEAR LORD WISBEACH,

May I so far trespass on your good nature as to ask
for your votes for a candidate for admission to the Infant
Orphan School at Winford, of which I see you are a governor. I fear my slight acquaintance with you hardly
justifies me in making this request, but if it is in your
power to grant it, I trust you will do so. You will judge,
from the enclosed particulars, of the merits of the case.

> Believe me, dear Lord Wisbeach,
> Very truly yours,
> MAUDE FAIRLEIGH.

From a Lady to a Gentleman, asking for his Votes.

MRS. LONSDALE is greatly interested in obtaining
admission for a little girl to the Mayfield Orphan
Asylum, and ventures to ask Mr. Boyd for his votes
for the May election if not already promised. This is a
most pitiful case, and Mrs. Lonsdale hopes that she may
be so fortunate as to obtain Mr. Boyd's support, and en-
closes the card and all particulars.

> DALE HOUSE, COLCHESTER,
> *February 17th.*

From a Lady asking for a Subscription.

> LONGFIELD, NORWOOD,
> *December 18th,* 18—.

DEAR MR. ALLISON,

I know how generous you are in subscribing to any
·erving charity, and I also know how many are the
ns made upon you for assistance; but I still venture

to ask for a subscription for our Infirmary, which is very much in need of support. I will only add, the Institution is a most excellent one, and that I should be very grateful for any donation, however small, as there is a great deal of illness about just now, and the Infirmary is not equal to the demands made upon it. I take the greatest interest in this charity, and am doing all I can amongst my friends in its behalf.

Believe me,
Very truly yours,
JULIA FRYER.

From a Lady to a Clergyman respecting an application for Assistance.

GREENWOOD, IPSWICH.

DEAR SIR,
Would you be kind enough to tell me if you know anything of Mrs. Parker; she has applied to me for assistance, but I make a point, if possible, of ascertaining how far the person applying for help is deserving of it, as I do not approve of indiscriminate charity, considering it is likely to do more harm than good. Perhaps I had better send you her letter, and if you have no personal knowledge of her, would you oblige me by making inquiries in your village ?

Believe me,
Very truly yours,
GRACE MEADOWS.

From a Gentleman to a Clergyman, asking him to visit his Mother.

8, ST. JOHN'S VILLAS, BARNES,
April 10th, 18—.

DEAR SIR,
My mother is very seriously ill, and begs me to say it would be a great comfort to her if you would come and see her, and read a little with her, if you could spare the time. In any case, I should be very glad to think she had seen you as it is her great wish to do so.

Faithfully yours,
GEORGE BRYCE.

To the Rev. JAMES WILSON.

From a Gentleman to a Clergyman, requesting his immediate presence.

10, CAMPDEN PLACE, W.
December 14th, 18—.

DEAR SIR,

Will you do me the favour to come round immediately for the purpose of baptising our little boy, who has just been given over, and we are very anxious to have him baptised, I fear there is not the faintest hope of his recovery.

Faithfully yours,
HENRY LLOYD.

To the REV. MR. BROOKE.

From a Lady to a Clergyman respecting a School Treat.

THE FIRS, FULHAM,
August 24th, 18—.

DEAR SIR,

I understand from one of your parishioners, Mrs. Fulbourne, that you propose giving a Sunday School treat to the children of your schools, I shall have much pleasure in placing my grounds and the adjoining field at your disposal for that purpose, and I shall be happy to provide a substantial tea for the teachers and those ladies connected with the schools. With compliments to yourself and Mrs. Jennings,

Believe me,
Yours very truly,
ADELAIDE BARCOMBE.

To the REV. — JENNINGS.

To a Gentleman, asking him to act as Reference.

16, BLANDFORD GARDENS, W.
July 14th, 18—.

DEAR MR. ROBERTS,

I have taken a furnished house at Balham for a year and am required to give two references. As you have known me for many years I thought perhaps you would kindly allow me to refer the agent to you. I referred him to my brother-in-law in the first instance.

I hope Mrs. Roberts is pretty well, please remember me to her and believe me,

Very truly yours,
M. E. KELLY.

From a Gentleman giving a Reference.

LUDLOW HOUSE, HIGHGATE,
March 1st, 18—.

DEAR SIRS,

In reply to your letter I beg to say I have known Mrs. Kelly for many years, and consider her to be a most responsible person and a highly desirable tenant.

Faithfully yours,
DONALD ROBERTS.

Messrs. WILSON & BROWN.

From a Lady to a Solicitor, asking Advice.

FERN LODGE, CHRISTCHURCH, HANTS.
April 3rd, 18—

DEAR SIR,

I am in a little difficulty respecting a late servant of mine. I dismissed her for misconduct without giving her a month's warning; she has now summoned me for a month's wages; what would you advise me to do in the matter? Perhaps you will kindly drop me a line.

With compliments,

Yours truly,
EMMA BATES.

To W. ROSS, ESQ.

From a Lady to a Solicitor respecting a Claim.

3, CUMBERLAND GARDENS, W.
July 6th, 18—.

DEAR SIR,

I enclose a letter received this morning from Messrs. Barnes, Mr. White's solicitors, asking for compensation for damage done to his brougham by its coming into collision with my victoria. I will send my coachman to you to-morrow morning that he may explain the nature of the accident, and I think you will see that no blame attaches to him. Will you have the goodness after you have seen him to write to Messrs. Barnes to this effect?

Believe me,
Yours very truly,
LOUISA TURNER.

To S. TANNER, ESQ.

From a Lady to a Solicitor, requiring his attendance upon a Relative.

8, SOUTH CRESCENT, REGENT'S PARK,
February 14*th*, 18—,

DEAR SIR,
I am desired by my father to ask you if you will
kindly come and see him this afternoon on urgent private
business; he seems very anxious to see you, and begged
me to lose no time in sending for you.

Faithfully yours,
To H. BARKER, ESQ. MARIAN BURGESS.

**From a Lady to a Medical Man, requesting his imme-
diate attendance.**

VERNON VILLA, UPPER NORWOOD,
March 29*th*, 18—.

DEAR MR. BELL,
My daughter is suffering from a severe sore throat.
I shall be glad if you will call and see her this morning.
I feel very anxious about her; I am afraid I ought to have
sent for you yesterday.

Very truly yours,
MARY BOYCE.

From a Lady to a Medical Man, requesting him to call.

March 29*th*, 18—.

MRS. GRAHAM presents her compliments to Dr.
Brooke and will feel greatly obliged if he will come and
see her little boy, who seems very feverish and unwell, and
she is afraid his illness may prove a serious one.

CLARENCE VILLA,
MAIDA VALE.

From a Lady to a Medical Man, asking for his account.

May 1*st*, 18—.

MRS. GRAHAM presents her compliments to Dr. Bell,
and wishes to know the amount she is indebted to him for
his attendance on her little boy, as she is going into the
country immediately for some months.

CLARENCE VILLA,
MAIDA VALE.

From a Lady to a Professor of Music.

MRS. COLE would be obliged if Signor Ronti would let her know his terms for a course of twelve lessons at her own residence; perhaps Signor Ronti would make it convenient to call upon her any morning during this week before 12 o'clock, when he would be able to judge of the progress her daughter has already made.

3, CAVENDISH PLACE, W.,
July 21st, 18—.

From a Professor of Music to a Lady.

SIGNOR RONTI presents his compliments to Mrs. Cole and begs to say that his terms are one guinea per lesson; he makes no reduction for a course of lessons. He will have the honour of calling on Mrs. Cole on Wednesday morning at 11.30.

10, TAVISTOCK STREET, S.W.,
July 22nd, 18—.

From a Lady to an Artist respecting her Daughter's Portrait.

18, BEAUMONT SQUARE, S.W.

MRS. ALLISON is very desirous of having a portrait of her daughter painted by Mr. Harvey. Will he therefore kindly appoint the most convenient hour to receive her at his studio, when the price of the portrait, the number of sittings to be given, and other details can be discussed.

Tuesday, March 7th, 18—.

To a Friend, requesting a Loan.

5, SYDNEY VILLAS, TULSE HILL,
December 18th, 18 —.

MY DEAR THOMPSON,

I have a great favour to ask you, which I hope you will be able to grant. I have a most pressing need for £30. Do you think you could oblige me with that sum for a couple of months, when I would punctually repay you? I feel the greatest reluctance in making this request,

c

and only the extreme urgency of the case induces me to do
so, although I feel that if it is in your power to serve me in
this I may count upon your friendship.

> Believe me, dear Thompson,
> Ever yours,
> H. PETERS.

From a Lady to a Relative, asking for a Loan.

> THE DOWER HOUSE, UXBRIDGE,
> *December 3rd,* 18—.

MY DEAR MARY,

I am in great anxiety at the present moment, being
unexpectedly called upon to pay a heavy bill of costs to
my solicitors, which they claim to my great astonishment.
It amounts to £68, and they ask for this amount within
ten days. I am quite unable to meet this heavy sum just
now, and I write to ask if you would be so very kind as
to lend me £25 towards it.

You may depend upon my repaying you as soon as I
receive my dividends, although they are, as you know,
painfully inadequate to my many expenses, which renders
this, may I say, extortionate demand the harder to submit
to; but in the hands of a solicitor one feels helpless and
powerless. At least this is my experience of the profession.

I so trust you may be able to grant my request. I shall
be sincerely grateful to you for any assistance you can give
me.

> Believe me,
> Your affectionate cousin,
> LUCY RICE.

From a Lady asking a Friend to enquire about a Furnished House.

> HILL HOUSE, TORQUAY,
> *April 10th,* 18—.

DEAR MRS. BARNETT,

We are thinking of coming to town for a couple of
months if we can find a small house to suit us.

Messrs. Roberts, House Agents, have sent me several
particulars of houses, which they highly recommend.

Would you be so very kind as to go over and examine two

houses for me for which I have received orders to view, and tell me your opinion of them, whether they are fairly well furnished, and thoroughly clean—I mean as regards bedding, &c.

They ask a very moderate rent, 4 guineas per week—so that I do not expect too much in the way of furniture and carpets, and I shall be satisfied if you could give a favourable report as to the general condition of things in either of these houses.

It would be a real favour if you would do this for me, as I am anxious to avoid the long journey to town that attending to this matter personally would entail.

With kind regards, and hoping we shall soon meet,

Believe me,

Very truly yours,

H. SUMMERS.

To a Lady, asking her to engage Apartments.

20, CATHEDRAL STREET, NORWICH,
July 5th, 18—.

DEAR MRS. HALE,

We propose spending a few weeks at Boulogne, and I should much prefer taking apartments to going to an hotel. I thought perhaps you might be able to recommend us some rooms where we should be comfortable. If not, would you mind the trouble of making a few inquiries?

We should like to face the sea if possible, and should require a sitting-room and three bed-rooms. I suppose the rent would be about four guineas per week.

Should you see any rooms likely to suit, would you engage them for us from the 1st of August for four weeks certain? I fear the town will be very full, and that without your help we should have no little difficulty on arrival in securing rooms.

I hope we shall have fine weather during our stay at Boulogne, and that we shall see a great deal of you all.

With our united kind regards, believe me,

Very sincerely yours,

H. BROOKE.

From a Lady, asking a Friend to make a Purchase for her.

Ivy House, Taunton,
April 27th, 18—.

My dear Miss Lacey,

May I ask you to execute a little commission for me?

I want to buy a really nice mantle, and I have no idea what people are wearing just now. I seldom go to town, as you know, and there are no fashions to study in these parts; indeed, we are very primitive as regards dress, and I do not like to trust entirely to fashion-books, for fear of ordering something exaggerated in style.

Your taste is so good, and you know exactly what is most suitable to my figure and height, that I should feel more than satisfied if you would choose a mantle for me at about 8 guineas, for which I enclose a little cheque.

Have you been buying anything pretty this spring? I know you are a great authority on dress, and I suppose you brought home some smart gowns from Paris. Are the bonnets as pointed as ever? and what will be the favourite colour this season?

We are as usual very quiet down here; but I am going to pay a few visits in Hampshire next month.

Believe me, dear Miss Lacey,
Affectionately yours,
H. Phillips.

From a Lady in India respecting a Home for her Children.

Calcutta,
March 24th, 18—.

My dear Mrs. Graham,

You were such an old friend of my dear mother's, that I trust you still take a little interest in me and mine.

I am sorry to say there is no chance of our returning home at present, and I am advised to send my two darling children to England with as little delay as possible. I have seen several advertisements in the Indian papers relating to homes for children, and I have selected two out of the number which appear to answer my requirements; but as placing my almost infants in the care of a stranger occasions me no little anxiety, I should be truly glad if you, dear Mrs. Graham, would make personal inquiries respecting the homes offered in the accompanying advertisements, and I hope you will allow me to defray any expenses incurred in complying with my request. I only wish you could tell me of some acquaintance of your own who would take charge of my darlings for a few years, and from whom they would receive a mother's care.

I am anxious to send this letter by this evening's mail, which must be my excuse for not writing a longer one.

With kindest remembrances from my husband and myself, believe me,

Very sincerely yours,

E. WILLETT.

From a Gentleman in India to a Friend in England, asking him to show Civility to a Family returning thither.

DEHRA ISMAIL KHAN, PUNJAUB,
February 24th, 18—.

MY DEAR LLOYD,

Since writing to you I find some great friends of mine, Mr. and Mrs. Darcy, are going to England immediately; he is on sick leave, having had a bad attack of low fever. They talk of spending the greater part of the time in your neighbourhood.

It seems he was born near Denbigh, and he has an idea that his native air will do great things for him. I hope it may, poor fellow.

If you have an opportunity of showing them any civility I am sure they would appreciate it; I have received much kindness from both him and his wife since I came out, which I think will induce you to give them a kind welcome. I trust you are all well at home. Please remember me to Mrs. Lloyd, and believe me,

Very truly yours,

C. ROBERTS.

From a Gentleman to the English Ambassador at a Foreign Court, requesting a Presentation.

MR. WHELAND begs to solicit the honour of a presentation to His Majesty the King of Spain, through the kind offices of His Excellency Sir Stanley Mortimer.

Mr. Wheland was presented at the Court of St. James's by Sir John Devine, on Feb. 23rd, 1875.

HOTEL INGLATERRA, MADRID,
January 3rd, 18—.

From the Secretary of an English Ambassador at a Foreign Court relative to a Presentation.

BRITISH EMBASSY, MADRID,
January 4th, 18—.

SIR,

I am directed by Sir Stanley Mortimer to acknowledge the receipt of your letter of yesterday's date, requesting the honour of presentation to His Majesty the King of Spain, and I beg to inform you in reply, that your name has been entered on the list for presentation at the Spanish Court on the next opportunity.

I remain, Sir,
Yours obediently,
HORACE CLIFFORD,
Secretary to H. M.'s Embassy.

MR. WHELAND,
Hotel Inglaterra.

From a Lady, asking for an Invitation to a Ball for a Friend.

18, ONSLOW TERRACE, S.W.,
March 24th, 18—.

DEAR MRS. VANE,

If your invitation list is not already filled up, might I ask you if you would give me a card for Miss Allen, the daughter of a very old friend of mine? She much wishes for an invitation to your ball, and I have promised to ask you this favour. Should you be able to grant it I would bring her with me.

I must apologise for trespassing on your kindness in this matter, but you will not hesitate to refuse if your list is already overfull as regards ladies.

Believe me,
Very truly yours,
H. VANDALEUR.

From a Lady declining to give an Invitation.

17, GUILDFORD SQUARE, S.W.,
May 25th, 18—.

DEAR MRS. VANDELEUR,

I am sorry to say my ball list is quite filled up; indeed I have been obliged to leave out many of my own acquaintances I should wish to have included.

Should I have any refusals at the last moment I will let you know, but I fear there is very little chance of this.

Believe me,
Very truly yours,
G. VANE.

From a Lady asking for an Invitation to a Ball for a Gentleman.

32, BRYANSTONE PLACE,
May 30th, 18—.

DEAR MRS. GRAHAM,

Would you mind asking Mr. Ernest Lovel to your ball? He said he should be charmed to go to it if I could get him a card, and as he is very fond of dancing I thought he might be an acquisition if you are short of gentlemen.

I think you have met his married sister, Mrs. Montague, at my house. I am very intimate with her.

Believe me,
Very sincerely yours,
G. BENNETT.

Asking for an Invitation to Amateur Theatricals.

18, CLARENDON CRESCENT, W.,
May 18th, 18—.

DEAR MRS. PIGOT,

Mr. and Mrs. Churchill, of Ellesmere Grange, Hants, who are old friends of mine, are up in town just now, and have heard so much of your forthcoming theatricals that if you could spare them a card, I know they would greatly appreciate it. They are staying at the Queen's Hotel, and if you are able to give them an invitation, perhaps you would kindly send it direct to them to save time?

Believe me,
Very sincerely yours,
C. NEWTON.

To the Superintendent of the Luggage Department concerning Lost Luggage.

THE HAND HOTEL, LLANGOLLEN,
August 24th, 18—.

SIR,

On arriving here from Cambridge last evening by the 7.20 train, I found that a large leather portmanteau was missing from amongst my luggage. I left Cambridge by the 9.20 train and saw my luggage labelled for Llangollen, and at Bletchley where I changed, I remember seeing this particular portmanteau on the platform with my other luggage. On changing again at Stafford, I discovered it was missing. The station-master undertook to telegraph to Bletchley, but up to the present moment I have heard nothing of it.

Will you make inquiries respecting it at Cambridge and Bletchley, and have it forwarded without delay? It bears my initial letters, C. B., and is also labelled, "Passenger to Llangollen."

I am, Sir,

Yours faithfully,

CHARLES BOND.

To the Superintendent of the Luggage Department concerning Lost Luggage.

5, MONTPELIER CRESCENT, BRIGHTON,
August 4th, 18—.

To the Superintendent.

SIR,

I left London Bridge station for Brighton by the 4.30 train this afternoon, and on arriving at the Brighton station I found that a large wicker basket was missing from amongst my luggage.

I saw my luggage weighed and labelled at London Bridge and in charge of a porter five minutes before the train started. I have therefore to complain of great negligence on his part.

The basket bears my name and address in full, with the words, "Passenger to Brighton," written on a parchment label; the contents are perishable, and if I do not receive it to-morrow morning I shall certainly demand compensation from the Company.

I am, Sir,

Yours faithfully,

GERTRUDE BIRD.

CHAPTER III.

From a Gentleman applying for a Secretaryship.

SACKVILLE HOUSE, BARNES,
December 18th, 18—.

GENTLEMEN,
I understand that the post of Secretary to the Dawlish Mining Company is about to become vacant, and I beg to make an application for the same. I enclose my testimonials, and trust they may be found satisfactory. I may add, that I am a good accountant, and have a foreign knowledge of French and German.
I have the honour to remain, Gentlemen,
Faithfully yours,
HENRY G. BAGOTT.

To the DIRECTORS OF THE DAWLISH MINING COMPANY.

From a Gentleman asking for a Clerkship for his Son.

18, PELHAM SQUARE, W.,
December 8th, 18—.

MY DEAR LINDLEY,
I have a great favour to ask you, and I hope you will grant it if it is in your power. I am very anxious to obtain a clerkship for my son in a public office. He is now 16, and is a clever, intelligent young fellow. Could you put his name down for a junior clerkship in your office? I should be most grateful to you if you could give him this start in life; he has his way to make in the world, and cannot begin too early. I have given him a sound education, and I think I may promise he would do your recommendation credit. Will you turn this matter over in your

mind, and let me hear from you in the course of a few
days?

Very truly yours,

G. BARKER.

From a Lady asking for a Clerkship for her Son.

6, CLARENDON TERRACE, REGENT'S PARK,

January 14*th*, 18—.

DEAR MR. ROBARTS,

May I so far trespass on your kindness as to ask
you to interest yourself in my son? I am very desirous of
obtaining a clerkship for him, and thought perhaps if a
vacancy occurred in your Bank you would kindly remember him. Although I am aware you must have many
applications of this nature, I cannot resist taking the
chance of its being in your power to do sometihng for him
in this way. He is 17 years of age, and has been educated
in Germany, which may be in his favour, as he is considered
a good linguist. I need not say how grateful I should be if
you would consider this request.

Believe me,

Very truly yours,

H. G. LAWRENCE.

Applying for a Situation of Clerk in answer to an Advertisement.

18, TULSE HILL TERRACE, BRIXTON,

January 4*th*, 18—.

SIR,

I see in the " Times " of this morning that you are
advertising for a junior clerk, and I beg to apply for the
situation. I have been twelve months in the house of
Messrs. Hawkins & Bush, 18, Gate Street, E.C., as a
junior clerk, and I can therefore refer you to them as to
my respectability and fitness for the post. I am 19 years
of age, and thoroughly understand book-keeping by double
entry, and the usual routine of office work. My late father
was for many years Manager of Messrs. Pryke & Johnson's
Patent Cement Works.

I beg to remain,

Yours obediently,

WILLIAM BARROW.

To MR. LAWSON.

Applying for a Situation in a Wholesale House of Business.

2, NORTH STREET, ISLINGTON,
January 17th, 18—.

SIR,

I beg to apply for the situation which I have heard is now vacant in your warehouse. I am 23 years of age, and have lived 18 months with Messrs. Scotches & Fortin, retail provision dealers, to whom I could refer you as to character and conduct should you entertain this application. I left them solely on account of their making a reduction in their establishment. Messrs. S. & F. had an extensive country connection, and I have therefore had some little experience in the prompt dispatch of large orders. I may mention the wages I received with them were   shillings per week.

I remain, yours obediently,
GEORGE BARNETT.

To MR. RIDDLE.

Applying for a Situation in a Retail Establishment.

18, RIVER STREET, WANDSWORTH,
January 18th, 18—.

SIR,

I am informed that you are in want of an experienced hand in the show-room department of your establishment. I have filled a similar situation with Mr. Lymes of King Street, for the last three years, who has promised me excellent references. I am desirous of obtaining a salary of £2 per week. Should this meet your views, and should you consider that I am likely to suit you, perhaps you would kindly favour me with a reply appointing an hour for me to call on you?

I remain, Sir,
Yours obediently,
ROBERT BATES.

To MR. KING.

From a Father applying for a Situation in a Retail House of Business for his Son.

5, KENT ROAD, TEDDINGTON,
June 24th, 18—.

SIR,

I much wish to place my son in a retail house of business, and I understand that you have an opening at the present moment for a lad. My boy is 16 years of age, writes a good hand, and is very quick at figures. As he has everything to learn, I should be willing to give his services for a twelvemonth in consideration of his being taken into the house and receiving full board.

Awaiting the favour of your reply,

I am, Sir,

Yours respectfully,

JAMES RICE.

To MR. PATTISON.

From a Young Lady applying for a Situation in a House of Business.

18, WEST STREET, HASTINGS,
September 14th, 18—.

MADAM,

I am most anxious to obtain a situation in a Fancy Repository. May I ask if there is likely to be a vacancy in your establishment, either in or out of the house? I have been apprenticed to the business for two years with Mrs. Young, who would be happy to recommend me, as she considers that I thoroughly understand the various branches of the fancy business, and am expert in the embroidery department.

I am, Madam,

Yours obediently,

MARY CHALLIS.

To MRS. HOLDEN.

To a Firm relative to an Apprenticeship.

5, SOUTH STREET, CAMBRIDGE,
January 3rd, 18—.

MADAM,

I write to ask if there is an opening in your house for an indoor apprentice, and in that case what would be the amount of premium required. I wish to apprentice my daughter to the dressmaking business. She is 13 years of age, and works very neatly. I could not afford to give a high premium, as my late husband left me in very straitened circumstances.

> I beg to remain, Madam,
> Yours obediently,
> E. CROSS.

To MRS. GRANT.

From a Clerk, asking a former Employer to act as Reference.

> SYDNEY VILLA, PECKHAM,
> *November 29th, 18—.*

GENTLEMEN,

I am about to obtain a responsible situation in the house of Messrs. Jaggard & Allen; they have asked me to furnish two references of commercial standing, and having lived with you for three years I ventured to give the name of your firm in addition to that of my late employer. May I trust that you will say all you can in my favour?

> I beg to remain, Gentlemen,
> Yours obediently,
> SAMUEL NASH.

To MESSRS CLAYTON & CO.

To a Gentleman recommending a Clerk.

> 200, BRIDGE STREET, E.C.,
> *December 18th, 18—.*

DEAR SIR,

I have much pleasure in recommending Mr. H. Wood for the post of clerk, and beg to say that I found him while in my service thoroughly trustworthy, quick, and intelligent; his general conduct left nothing to be desired.

> I am, Sir,
> Faithfully yours,
> J. BROWN.

To H. BROOKE, Esq.

Applying for the character of a Clerk.

205, CHEAPSIDE,
December 16th, 18—.

DEAR SIR,

I understand Mr. H. Wood has been a clerk in your house for the last twelve months. I am thinking of engaging him should his references prove satisfactory. Will you therefore kindly inform me if you consider him thoroughly trustworthy and reliable?

I am, Sir,

Faithfully yours,

H. BROOKE.

To J. BROWN, Esq.

Applying for the Situation of Manager at an Hotel.

ARGUS CLUB, ST. JAMES' STREET,
July 7th, 18—.

To the Proprietor of the Grand Hotel, S.W.

SIR,

I beg to apply for the situation of Manager at your hotel, which I am informed will shortly become vacant. The fact of my having been steward of the Argus Club for the last 7 years will, I venture to hope, influence you in my favour, and several gentlemen on the committee have kindly promised to recommend me, and to speak favourably as to my management of the Club and general integrity of conduct.

Previous to being steward of the Argus Club, I was head waiter at the Mitre Hotel, Oxford, for over five years, and the proprietor of that establishment would also give me the highest recommendation.

Perhaps I had better mention that the salary I feel justified in asking is £150 per annum, with full board.

Should you entertain this application, I should be happy to wait upon you at any hour you may appoint, and beg to remain, Sir,

Yours faithfully,

JOHN GLOVER.

Answer to an Advertisement for a Companion and Chaperon.

MANOR HOUSE, KEW.
May 4th, 18—.

SIR,

In reply to your advertisement for a "Companion and Chaperon to a young lady," I venture to offer myself for the post.

My late husband had an appointment in Somerset House; I am 27 years of age, and have been a widow three years. I am a good linguist, and can speak French and German fluently; so that should your daughter wish to continue her studies or to travel, my knowledge of languages might be of use to her. I am considered a clever musician, and have had a good musical education. The salary mentioned in your advertisement would be quite satisfactory to me, and I should consider myself most fortunate were my qualifications to meet with your approval.

With regard to references, Mrs. White, wife of the Rev. E. White, Grafton Rectory, Colchester, and Mrs. Bruce, 17, Lansdown Square, S.W., would be very happy to answer any questions respecting me.

Believe me, dear Sir,
Yours faithfully,
H. ROBINS.

Answer to an Advertisement for a Useful Companion.

17, WIMBORNE PLACE, BLOOMSBURY,
July 10th, 18—.

MADAM,

In answer to your advertisement in the *Times* of Saturday the 7th inst., I beg to offer my services as "Useful Companion to an Elderly Lady." I should not be afraid to undertake the care of an invalid, and to have the management of household affairs, as in both these particulars I have had no little experience in my own family. I am 36 years of age, and the daughter of a medical man. Owing to circumstances with which I need not trouble you at the present moment, I am anxious to obtain a situation of this nature.

I have been accustomed to read aloud and to write letters from dictation, and to amuse elderly people.

Perhaps it is premature to mention references in this letter, but I may say that I could thoroughly satisfy you on this point by referring you to several ladies who have kindly promised to recommend me.

I am, Madam,

Yours faithfully,

G. E. BARNES.

To a Lady making Inquiries about a School.

5 DUDLEY TERRACE, W.,

June 18th, 18—.

DEAR MRS. RYDER,

May I ask you a few questions respecting a school kept by Miss Wrexham at Hastings, as I understand your little girl is one of her pupils? Are you thoroughly satisfied with the system of education followed at this school, and are the domestic arrangements with regard to comfort and living all that you could wish? My little girl is rather delicate and requires care. Do you think she would be happy in Miss Wrexham's charge, and is your daughter likely to remain with her beyond this term? I should feel grateful for any particulars you could give me on this to me most important subject, and I hope you will kindly excuse my troubling you with these inquiries.

Believe me,

Very truly yours,

E. J. JENNINGS.

To a Lady giving an unfavourable opinion about a School.

7, CLARENCE GARDENS, W.,

June 20th, 18—.

DEAR MRS. JENNINGS,

You ask if my daughter is to remain at Hastings beyond this term. I am seriously thinking of having her home at once, as she has not been at all well lately, and I doubt if the confinement of school hours altogether agrees with her. I can hardly express an opinion with respect to the progress she has made in her studies, as she has been there so short a time. I believe the living is fairly good, but as you know, delicate children require especial care and attention. Miss Wrexham's school was not personally recommended to me by any friend of mine, I heard of it simply through an advertisement.

Believe me,
Very truly yours,
G. L. RYDER.
_____

From a Lady recommending a Governess.

CAVENDISH HOUSE, RICHMOND,
June 22nd, 18—.

DEAR MRS. FAIRFAX,

I am able to speak in the highest terms of Miss Robins, both as regards her capabilities and moral training; she has been carefully brought up and well educated; is amiable and high principled. She speaks German and French fluently, and her knowledge of music is above the average; she has acquired some experience in teaching, through having instructed her younger sisters. I may add from what I know of Miss Robins you need have no hesitation in engaging her.

Believe me,
Very truly yours,
B. H. MORGAN.
_____

From a Governess applying for a Situation.

9, CHEPSTOW PLACE, RICHMOND,
June 20th, 18—.

MADAM,

I heard from Mrs. Morgan this morning that you were in want of a governess for your two little girls, and she recommended me to apply for the situation at once, thinking that I might perhaps suit you. My experience in teaching has been gained at home; for the last two years I have undertaken the sole tuition of my younger sisters. I may say that I have been well educated myself, and am quite capable of instructing young ladies up to the age of fourteen. Mrs. Morgan has known my family for many years, and begs me to say that should you wish her to write to you respecting my qualifications and fitness for the post of governess in your house, she will be happy to do so.

I remain, Madam,
Very truly yours,
G. ROBINS.

D

From a Governess asking a Lady to be her Reference.

5, St. Peter's Terrace, S.W.,
December 8th, 18—,

Dear Madam,

Would you kindly allow me to refer to you as having known me when governess in Mrs. Martin's family? I cannot unfortunately obtain her address, as she is still travelling on the continent. Mrs. Flower, of 18, Stanhope Terrace, is willing to engage me as governess to her little girl if my references are satisfactory, and in the absence of Mrs. Martin I venture to ask you this favour.

I remain, Madam,
Faithfully yours,
H. Ellis.

From a Lady acting as Reference for a Governess.

18, Park Terrace, W.

Mrs. Palmer begs to inform Mrs. Flower that her friend Mrs. Martin considered Miss Ellis to be a highly efficient governess, and had a sincere regard for her. Mrs. Palmer is able to endorse this opinion from personal observation and knowledge, and is quite sure that Mrs. Martin if in England would give Miss Ellis the highest possible recommendation.

December 10th, 18—.

To a Lady respecting the qualifications of a Governess.

Bandon Lodge,
June 28th, 18—.

Dear Mrs. Morgan,

You were kind enough to recommend Miss Robins to me as a governess for my little girls. I understand from her letter that she has not hitherto filled a similar situation, but this I should not consider a drawback, if her qualifications were satisfactory. Would you say she was thoroughly well educated? Can she teach French and German to beginners, and has she a good knowledge of music? Is she very amiable and conscientious? She says you have known her family for some years, so no doubt you will be able to satisfy me on all these points. As regards the question of salary, I propose giving my governess thirty guineas per annum. Will you kindly mention this to her, and if your answer is such as I expect it will be, I shall have no hesitation in engaging her at once. I have had a great many applications for this situation, but I think it such an advantage to obtain a governess personally recommended by a friend of one's own, therefore I am so much obliged to you for advising Miss Robins to write to me.

With kind remembrances, believe me, dear Mrs. Morgan,

Very truly yours,
M. E. FAIRFAX.

From a Lady in reply to an Advertisement for a Housekeeper.

8, QUEEN'S ROAD, HORNSEY,
December 3rd, 18—.

SIR,

In answer to your advertisement in this morning's *Times* for a housekeeper, I beg to offer my services in that capacity.

I am 35 years of age, and my experience has been gained through having had the entire control of my uncle's house for seven years. The whole of the domestic arrangements were in my hands. The engaging and dismissing the servants, giving all orders, and keeping the household accounts. I also superintended the education of the two younger children, attended to their wardrobes, and had the entire charge of them.

I can offer two unexceptionable references, besides a personal one from my uncle, Mr. Perth, 5, Finsbury Park, N.

I have no doubt that you will receive many applications for the situation vacant in your establishment, still I venture to hope that this offer of my services may meet with your favourable consideration.

I am, Sir,
Faithfully yours,
H. PARTRIDGE.

Applying for a Situation of Working Housekeeper.

NORTH STREET, UPPER HOLLOWAY,
January 25th, 18—.

SIR,
I understand from Mr. Brown, fishmonger, of Sydney Street, that you are in want of a working house-keeper, and I beg to apply for the situation, as I think I could thoroughly perform the duties you require.

Since the death of my husband, three years ago, I have had the management of a lodging-house at Brighton; it was a very responsible situation, and I may add that I gave complete satisfaction. I mention this that you may understand my fitness to superintend and assist in all household work, including cooking.

I am informed that the wages you offer are £30 per annum, with everything found.

I can furnish you with two or three excellent references as to character, should you think fit to entertain this application.

I am, Sir,
Yours obediently,
SUSAN ARMSTRONG.

Applying for the Situation of Housekeeper at an Hotel.

17, LATIMER ROAD, N.W.,
September 9th, 18—.

To the Manager.
SIR,
I understand that the situation of housekeeper at your hotel will become vacant next month, and I hasten to offer my services in that capacity, and from the nature of my former occupation, I trust you may consider me eligible. I have assisted my father for many years in the manage-ment of a large boarding-house at Hastings, and thoroughly understand the duties in every detail that would be required from a housekeeper at an hotel.

If you would allow me to call upon you, I could satisfy you as to my knowledge of the various domestic depart-ments that would come within the province of house-keeper.

I am 32 years of age, and am unmarried.

With regard to salary, I consider I should be entitled to ask £50 per annum, full board, and laundress expenses.

I enclose two recommendations, which perhaps you will do me the favour to look at.

Awaiting your reply,

I am, Sir,

Faithfully yours,

JANE MARTIN.

Applying for a Situation as Matron.

CATERHAM, SURREY,
May 13*th*, 18—.

SIR,

I beg to apply for the situation of matron at the St. Ann's Orphan Asylum, advertised as being vacant in the *Times* of this morning.

I am 43 years of age, and have filled a situation for the last 8 years as superintendent of the dormitories in St. Mary's School for girls, and was also one of the wardrobe keepers in the same establishment, and I thoroughly understand the routine of management requisite in an institution of this nature.

I enclose three testimonials as to character and capabilities, and trust that you may be induced to give this application your favourable consideration.

I am, Sir,

Yours obediently,

HARRIET RICHARDS.

To the SECRETARY OF THE ST. ANNE'S ORPHAN ASYLUM.

Giving a Testimonial to a Person applying for a Situation as Matron.

May 10*th*, 18—.

MRS. CROSS is able to speak in the highest terms of Harriet Richards from a personal knowledge extending over 5 years. She considers her thoroughly trustworthy and conscientious, and well-fitted for the post of matron from the experience she has acquired in a former employment. She is firm, judicious, and kind-hearted, and is very methodical and punctual in the performance of her duties.

GROVE HOUSE, LEWISHAM.

From a Young Lady applying for a Situation as Bookkeeper.

5, CANTERBURY ROAD, N.W.,
December 14th, 18—.

SIR,

In answer to your advertisement in the *Times* of Saturday the 13th inst. for a young lady to act as book-keeper, I beg to apply for the situation. I am 18 years of age, and have assisted my father during the last 4 years in keeping his books. I am quick at figures, and am a good accountant. I should be very glad to offer my services for a month on trial, that you might judge of my capabilities and general intelligence.

Mrs. Willis, of 5, Waterloo Street, will answer any questions respecting me. She has known me for some years.

I am, Sir,
Yours obediently,

To the MANAGER.   H. EVANS.

From a Lady applying for the character of a Lady's Maid.

5, FITZROY GARDENS, W.

MRS. HONEYWOOD would be much obliged if Mrs. Newton would inform her whether Mary Brown thoroughly understands the duties of lady's maid and is a good dress-maker and hairdresser, also whether she considers her trustworthy and reliable. Mrs. Honeywood understands Mary Brown left Mrs. Newton's service by her own desire, and that she is willing to give her a good character.

January 8th, 18—.

From a Lady recommending a Lady's Maid.

IN reply to Mrs. Honeywood's letter Mrs. Newton begs to say that she is able to answer all her questions satisfactorily respecting Mary Brown; she is a very good lady's maid, and well up in her duties, she can cut out and make dresses, and is very clever at dressing hair, and is most trustworthy in every way. Mrs. Newton was sorry to part with her, and she left her service owing to a disagreement with one of the servants.

17, MUNSTER SQUARE, W.,
January 14th, 18—

From a Lady applying for the character of a Maid-servant.

LANSDOWNE GRANGE.

WILL Mrs. Green kindly inform Mrs. Brand whether she considers Eliza Smith—who lived with her as house-maid—to be strictly honest, steady, obliging, and in all respects a good servant, also the reason of her leaving Mrs. Green's service?

January 10th, 18—.

From a Lady respecting the character of a Housemaid.

6, BANGOR VILLAS, SURBITON.

MRS. GREEN begs to say that Eliza Smith is honest and steady, but would require no little training before she could be considered a good servant. She was only in her service a very short time, and Mrs. Green parted with her, not finding her equal to the work expected from her.

January 12th, 18—.

To a Lady respecting the character of a Man-servant.

EAST CLIFFE HOUSE, FOLKESTONE,
June 3rd, 18—.

MADAM,

William Jones has applied to me for the situation of butler, stating that he lived with you in that capacity. Will you kindly tell me if while in your service he was steady, sober, honest, and whether he thoroughly understands his duties? He informs me he is not a married man. May I ask if this is the case as far as you know, and might I further ask the reason of your parting with him?

I am, Madam,
Faithfully yours,

To MRS. GARDNER.   G. BAKER.

From a Lady declining to give a Character.

18, HERTFORD PLACE, W.

MRS. GARDNER regrets to say that she must decline to give William Jones a character. She may further add that he was in her service five weeks only.

June 4th, 18—.

CHAPTER IV.

LETTERS RELATIVE TO ILLNESS AND DEATH.
ANNOUNCEMENTS AND CONDOLENCE.

To a Gentleman, announcing the Illness of his Wife.

5, VENTNOR TERRACE, BRIGHTON,
August 24th, 18—.

DEAR MR. BOND,

Although I am personally unknown to you, yet your wife is a great friend of mine, and I write to tell you I called this morning to see her and found that she was seriously ill. I am sure you ought to know of this at once, and I would have sent a telegram but the doctor said there was no immediate danger, and that I had better inform you of her illness by letter. The landlady of the lodgings where she is staying seems very attentive and kind, still I think it would be a great comfort to Mrs. Bond if you could bring her sister down with you. In the meantime I will do all I can for her, and I am happy to say she has the best advice the town can furnish.

I remain,
Yours sincerely,
M. GREENWAY.

To a Wife, announcing the Illness of her Husband.

WICKHAM HOUSE, ST. ALBANS,
September 18th, 18—.

DEAR MRS. YOUNG,

Your husband has asked me to write and tell you he has a bad attack of gout and cannot use his right arm; he feels quite helpless, and hopes you will come to him at once. We are taking every care of him, and he has a very good doctor, but of course he would be very glad to have you with him, and although we have not yet had the pleasure of meeting, I hope you will not make any

ceremony about staying with us until your husband is
quite well again. We shall be very pleased to see you in
spite of the unfortunate circumstance which occasions your
first visit to us.

Believe me,
Very truly yours,
G. L. MARRIOTT.

To a Married Daughter, announcing the Illness of her Mother.

WALLINGTON HOUSE, YORK,
November 25th, 18—.

DEAR MRS. BAKER,
I am sorry to tell you your mother has caught a
very severe cold, and the doctor seems anxious about her
and says it is an attack of bronchitis. She has been in bed
for the last three days, but would not let me write before
for fear of unnecessarily alarming you; however, to-day,
being no better, she has desired me to do so. The doctor is
coming again to-morrow, and should there be a change for
the worse I will send you a telegram after he has seen her.
She is very restless at night, and cannot be persuaded to
take any nourishment beyond a little milk. I came here
on a visit last week with the intention of returning home
yesterday, but I did not like to leave your mother as she
was so unwell.

With kind remembrances, believe me,
Very truly yours,
H. CLARKE.

From a Clerk to his Employers, excusing his absence on the ground of Illness.

1, GEORGE ST., N.E.,
April 2nd, 18—.

To Messrs. Brown.
GENTLEMEN,
I very much regret I was unable to attend at the
office this morning owing to a severe attack of illness. I
venture to enclose a certificate from the doctor who is
attending me, as he fears it will be several days before I
shall be able to resume my duties. I trust that my

enforced absence will not occasion you any serious inconvenience.

I beg to remain, Gentlemen,
Yours respectfully,
J. BLACK.

From a Widow, announcing the Death of her Husband to his late Employers.

ACACIA COTTAGE, PECKHAM,
December 20th, 18—.

GENTLEMEN,
I have to announce the death of my dear husband, which occurred last night after only three days' illness. Painful as it is to me to write to you under this terrible blow, I feel it my duty to inform you of it at once, on account of the position he occupied in your house.

I am, Gentlemen,
Yours respectfully,
H. CHAMBERLAIN.

To MESSRS. CRANSTOWN & WILLIS.

From a Daughter, announcing the Death of a Parent.

7, ENFIELD TERRACE, W.,
May 18th, 18—.

DEAREST AUNT,
You will, I fear, have been prepared for the sad intelligence I have to convey, the death of my dear mother. It took place yesterday afternoon. My father is too broken-hearted to write to you himself. We were all with her, and she was conscious up to the last. My father hopes my dear uncle will be able to attend the funeral on Saturday next. Excuse a longer letter to-day, dear aunt, as I am so very unhappy.

Your affectionate niece,
LAURA WHITE.

From a Lady to her Brother-in-law, announcing the Death of her Husband.

NEWPORT HOUSE, READING,
May 7th, 18—.

MY DEAR GEORGE,
You will have received my telegram telling you that my dear husband was sinking fast. The change for

the worse took place quite suddenly last night, and this morning at six o'clock he died. I am too miserable to write more, pray come to me at once if possible, there is so much to be arranged, and I feel quite unequal to giving the necessary directions for the funeral.

Your unhappy sister,
J. C. COURTNEY.

Offering to attend the Funeral of a Relative

5, WARWICK VILLAS, TEDDINGTON, ·
May 2nd, 18—.

DEAR AUNT BESSIE,

I cannot tell you how shocked and grieved I was to hear of my dear uncle's death. You did not say when the funeral is to take place, but please let me know, as I much wish to attend it and to pay this last mark of respect to one for whom I entertained so sincere an affection.

Believe me, dear Aunt,
Your affectionate nephew, ·
JAMES TURNER.

To a Relative, asking him to attend a Funeral.

THE GROVE, WESTFIELD,
April 6th, 18—.

MY DEAR UNCLE JOHN,

You will have received my telegram containing the sad intelligence of the death of my dear mother. My father is quite overcome with grief at the suddenness of the blow that has fallen upon us all, and is therefore unequal to writing to you himself, but he wishes me to say that the funeral is to take place on Saturday next, the 10th instant, at 2 o'clock, at the Westfield Cemetery, and he hopes you will attend if possible.

With our united best love, I remain,
Your affectionate nephew,
H. REYNOLDS.

Offering to attend the Funeral of a Friend.

17, EDINBURGH TERRACE, W.,
July 4th, 18—.

DEAR MRS. LUDLOW,

I was most grieved to hear of the death of my dear old friend Mr. Ludlow, and beg to offer you my sincere

sympathy. I much wish to attend the funeral, unless you
desire that only relatives should be present. Perhaps you
will kindly let me know your wishes on the subject, and
when and where the funeral is to take place.

I remain,
Very truly yours,
GEORGE WINTER.

Asking a Friend to attend a Funeral.

ST. JOHN'S VILLA, WIMBLEDON,
September 14th, 18—.

DEAR SIR,

I am desired by Mrs. Jones to inform you that the
funeral of her son, Mr. Edgar Jones, is appointed to take
place at St. Peter's Church, on Saturday, the 17th instant,
at 12 o'clock, and to say that she would be glad if you
would attend on the occasion.

I am, Sir,
Yours respectfully,
H. WHITEHEAD.

To a Gentleman, condoling with him on the Death of his Wife.

MONMOUTH HOUSE, WAKEFIELD,
July 3rd, 18—.

DEAR MR. BAGOT,

I hardly like to intrude upon you in your great
sorrow, but I cannot resist telling you how much my
husband and myself sympathise with you. We saw the
announcement of the death of your dear wife in the *Times,*
and were greatly shocked, as we had not even heard of her
illness. Pray do not think of answering this letter; I only
write to assure you how much we feel for you under this
severe bereavement, the more sad since your dear little
girls are thus deprived at so tender an age of a loving
mother's care.

With our united kind regards, believe me,

Very truly yours,
A. G. ANDREWS.

Condoling with a Lady on the Death of her Husband.

FORTESCUE HOUSE, NOTTING HILL,
July 23rd, 18—.

MY DEAR MRS. HOLMES,

I was deeply grieved to hear of the death of your husband, and write to offer you my sincerest sympathy. At present, I have no doubt, you can hardly realise your loss, and the blank made in your life must be very terrible to bear ; you were so much to each other, and appeared to be so truly happy in your married life. By-and-by I trust the care of your boy will give you an interest in life, but as yet I fear you must be too miserable to take comfort even from this.

With kind love, believe me
Your affectionate friend,
H. C. MASON.

To a Young Lady, condoling with her on the Death of her Mother.

GRANTHAM LODGE, EALING,
July 2nd, 18—.

MY DEAR BLANCHE,

I was most grieved to hear from you of the death of your dear mother, and I can well imagine how greatly you must miss her every hour. You have one consolation however, that of having been the best of daughters to her, and of having given her the most devoted care during her long illness. At such a time as this, little can be said to comfort you, and time alone will soften your sorrow for the loss of the kindest of mothers. I feel that I have lost a dear friend in her, and indeed all who knew her cannot fail to regret one who was so amiable and unselfish. Have you made any plans as yet, and what does your brother wish you to do?—are you to live with him or with one of your mother's relatives? I shall be very interested to hear what you propose doing, and if you would care to come to me for a quiet visit, do not hesitate to say so.

Believe me, dear Blanche,
Your affectionate friend,
H. L. BROOKE.

To a Lady, condoling with her on the Death of her Father-in-law.

6, PELHAM SQUARE, HASTINGS,
September 8th, 18—.

DEAR MRS. PETERS,

I see you have just lost your father-in-law; he was looking so well when I last saw him, that I was quite surprised and pained to hear of his death. Will you say everything that is most kind to your husband from me; I know how attached he was to his father, and I am afraid he will feel his loss very much. You and your children will also miss him greatly, he was so genial and kind-hearted, and such a charming old gentleman.

With love, believe me,
Very sincerely yours,
H. L. GARDNER.

Condoling with a Lady on the Death of her little Boy.

5, BEAUMONT TERRACE, BRIGHTON,
May 10th, 18—.

DEAR MRS. MONTAGUE,

I was truly sorry to hear of the loss you have sustained in the death of your dear little boy. Pray believe how sincerely I sympathise with you in your bitter sorrow. I feel how idle words must be to convey a shadow of comfort to your stricken heart, but yet it would seem unkind not to send you a few lines of heartfelt sympathy. I know how proud Mr. Montague was of his little son, and I can well imagine how he must grieve for him, and that the knowledge of his unhappiness must render this trial additionally hard for you to bear. I can only trust that in endeavouring to console him your mind may be, in a measure, diverted from dwelling upon your own grief.

With all kind wishes to you both, believe me,
Very sincerely yours,
A. C. RICKETTS.

To a Lady, condoling with her on the Death of her Brother.

18, GLASGOW TERRACE, REGENT'S PARK,
April 3rd, 18—.

MY DEAR MRS. ARKWRIGHT,

I was so sorry to hear of the death of your brother, as although you have not seen much of him of late years, still of course his death must have been a great shock to you. I remember him a fine, handsome young fellow; how sad that he should thus be cut off in the prime of life! Have you heard any particulars beyond the fact of his death? I suppose his poor young wife will return at once to England. I am truly grieved for you all, pray believe this, and with kind regards,

I remain always,
Your affectionate
G. E. SAUNDERS.

Condoling with a Lady on the Death of her Friend.

ROXBURGH GARDENS, DOVER,
January 28th, 18—.

DEAREST EDITH,

I only accidentally heard last night of the death of poor Mrs. Lawson; I know she was a great friend of yours, and you must have been very grieved when the intelligence reached you. You were so fond of her that no doubt you quite feel as if you had lost a near relation, and very naturally, as she was beloved and admired by all who knew her. I do so pity her husband, and the little motherless girl.

I hope you are pretty well; we have all been suffering from colds lately.

Believe me, dear Edith,
Your affectionate
MABEL CUNNINGHAM.

From a Husband in answer to a Letter of Condolence on the Death of his Wife.

8, TAVISTOCK TERRACE, W.
July 20th, 18—.

MY DEAR Mrs. ANDREWS,

Many thanks for your kind letter of sympathy. My dear wife's death has left me entirely miserable, and her loss to me is irreparable. She was the dearest and best of women, and the void left in my life is, indeed, most terrible to bear. My darling children are scarcely old enough to understand all the misery of the present moment.

Remember me kindly to your husband, and believe me,
Very truly yours,
J. BAGOT.

From a Wife in answer to a Letter of Condolence on the Death of her Husband.

17, TREVOR ROAD, W.,
August 2nd, 18—.

DEAR MRS. MASON,

Thank you much for your kind letter; the loss of my dear husband has left me unspeakably desolate, and I can hardly bear to write of my sorrow as yet. I feel too broken-hearted to do anything but sit down and cry helplessly. I know I ought to rouse myself, but the knowledge that he has gone from me for ever, and that henceforward I shall be alone, deprived of his loving care, is all that I can realise. By and by the duty I owe to my child will give me something to live for, but at present I can only mourn, and pray for resignation.

Believe me, dear Mrs. Mason,
Yours affectionately,
G. HOLMES.

To a Lady, in answer to Condolences on the Death of her little Boy.

8, STANHOPE TERRACE, RICHMOND,
May 15th, 18—.

DEAR MRS. RICKETTS,

I am very grateful for all your kind expressions of sympathy. I cannot tell you how deeply we both grieve for the death of our darling boy; perhaps it is selfish to wish him back again with us, but still how hard it is to lose him none but a mother's heart can say. My husband does not talk of his grief even to me, but I know the loss of our boy is a bitter trial to him; you see he was our only son, our great treasure; we had thought so much of his future, poor darling.

With our united kind regards believe me,
Very sincerely yours,
A. MONTAGUE.

To a Lady, returning thanks for Condolences on the Death of her Brother.

THE RED HOUSE, GUILDFORD,
April 8th, 18—.

MY DEAR MRS. SAUNDERS,

Very many thanks for your kind letter of condolence. My poor brother's unexpected death was indeed a great shock to us. All that we have as yet heard is that he was ill only three days, and that enteric fever was the cause of death; his wife was too overwhelmed with grief to write more fully, but we trust we shall hear from her by next mail. Her father is very anxious that she should return to England at once with her children. John and I were such great friends up to the time of his marriage, it seems too sad to think that I shall never see him again. I was so very fond and proud of him too, and his sudden death is so inexpressibly terrible to me.

With kind love believe me, dear Mrs. Saunders,

Yours affectionately,

M. E. ARKWRIGHT.

To a Lady who has offered her Condolences on the Death of a Friend.

6, CLARENDON GARDENS,
February 5th, 18—.

MY DEAR MABEL,

Poor Mrs. Lawson's death has indeed caused a blank amongst her many friends, but none of them will miss her more than I shall, as we were brought up together and were quite like sisters. I cannot tell you how greatly I feel her loss, she was so much to me in every way, such a dear dear friend. Her husband seems heart-broken, he thinks of going abroad for a few months, and his little daughter is to remain with me during his absence.

Excuse a longer letter to-day, and believe me, dear Mabel,

Your affectionate

EDITH CARTER.

To a Lady, inquiring after the Health of her Husband.

FAIRLIGHT LODGE, NR. DORKING,
April 4th, 18—.

MY DEAR MRS. HERBERT,

I sent over this morning to inquire after Mr. Herbert, and was very sorry indeed to hear he is no better, and that you are very anxious about him, but I trust there may be some improvement in his condition ere long. Pray do not think of answering this note; I merely write to assure you of my sympathy, and to say how glad I should

be if I could be of use to you in any way; I would of course come over at once if I thought you would care to see me.
With kindest regards,

Very sincerely yours,

ADA MORRIS.

To a Lady, indirectly inquiring after an Invalid.

ROYAL HOTEL, BATH,
June 2nd, 18—.

DEAR MRS. KING,

I accidentally heard yesterday through some friends who have just returned home, that your sister was seriously ill when they left Vichy; however, I hope that you have received a better report of her during the last few days, and that there is no further cause for anxiety. When you write will you say everything that is most kind from me, and please tell her I thought it best not to trouble her with a letter until I heard how she was, as I know how trying it is after a severe illness to answer letters of inquiry.

Believe me,

Yours most sincerely,

EVA WALDEN.

CHAPTER V.

OFFERING PRESENTS. THANKING FOR PRESENTS, &c.

To a Lady, enclosing Tickets for a Concert or Out-door Fête.

10, Sussex Gardens, S.W.,
July 24th, 18—.

Dear Miss Fletcher,

I venture to enclose two tickets for an Afternoon Concert at the Albert Hall on Tuesday next, in the hope that you may perhaps like to make use of them. It is to be a very good one, and well worth going to.

Please give my kind regards to Mrs. Fletcher, and believe me,

Faithfully yours,
Alfred Vernon.

From a Lady, accepting Tickets.

125, Seymour Place, W.,
July 26th, 18—.

Dear Mr. Vernon,

Thank you so much for the tickets just received. I shall be very pleased to go to the Concert at the Albert Hall on Tuesday next; unfortunately mamma is engaged on that day, but my aunt, Mrs. Gray, has promised to accompany me. Again thanking you,

Believe me,
Very truly yours,
Margaret Fletcher.

From a Lady, declining Tickets.

125, Seymour Place, W.,
July 26th, 18—.

Dear Mr. Vernon,

I cannot, I regret to say, make use of the tickets you were kind enough to send me, as I have a prior engagement

for Tuesday next; I therefore beg to return them with many
thanks.
> Believe me,
> Very truly yours,
> MARGARET FLETCHER.

To a Lady, offering a Bouquet.

> 5, LANDOVER GARDENS, S.W.,
> *December 3rd,* 18—.

DEAR MISS BRIDGEMAN,
  I should feel much gratified by your acceptance of
the accompanying bouquet. I have chosen red roses, as I
think you said you preferred them to any other flowers.
> Believe me,
> Very truly yours,
> EDWARD WARD.

To a Lady, offering a Song.

> EAST WOOD, WIMBLEDON,
> *July 3rd,* 18—.

DEAR MISS LESLIE,
  I venture to send you a new song I heard the other
evening, which I think perhaps you will like. I fancy it
will suit your voice very well, and I shall look forward to
the pleasure of hearing you sing it.
> Believe me,
> Very truly yours,
> GEORGE HOPWOOD.

From a Lady, acknowledging the Present of a Song.

> DAFFODIL COTTAGE, SURBITON,
> *July 4th,* 18—.

DEAR MR. HOPWOOD,
  Thank you very much for the song you were so kind
as to send me, I have tried it over and like it immensely.
I wonder if it was very well sung when you heard it, and
if I shall be able to do justice to it in your opinion, when I
have the pleasure of singing it to you.
> Believe me,
> Very sincerely yours,
> G. L. LESLIE.

To a Lady, offering a Birthday Present.

5, WORCESTER TERRACE, W.,
October 4th, 18—.

MY DEAR MISS OAKES,

I wish you very many happy returns of your birthday, and send you a little souvenir which I hope you will like ; at your age a birthday is an event to celebrate and to rejoice at, at mine it has a different signification, and reminds me that I am one year nearer the end, but in youth one does not dwell upon this thought, but rather upon what the bright future has in store. May it contain everything for you that your dearest friends could wish.

With love, believe me,
Your affectionate Friend,
J. L. PIERCE.

To a Lady, thanking her for a Birthday Present.

HEATH HOUSE, DERBY,
October 6th, 18—.

DEAR MRS. PIERCE,

I hardly know how to thank you for your handsome present, I was so surprised and delighted on receiving it. It was indeed kind of you to remember my birthday, and believe me I am most grateful for all your good wishes. I have had several very nice presents, but none that I shall value more than yours, dear Mrs. Pierce. We are to have a little dance to-night in honour of the event, so I shall have the pleasure of showing my birthday gifts to my particular friends.

With renewed thanks, believe me,
Affectionately yours.
HARRIET G. OAKES.

From a Stranger to an Invalid, offering Fruit and Flowers.

November 18th, 18—.

MRS. GRANTLY has the pleasure of sending Mrs. Norton some hot-house grapes, in the hope that they may be acceptable to her, as she understands Mrs. Norton is a great invalid ; she also sends her a few flowers, and trusts she will have no hesitation in accepting both with all good wishes for her restoration to health.

5, ROYAL CRESCENT, WEYMOUTH.

From a Lady to a Stranger, acknowledging a Present of Flowers and Fruit.

November 19th, 18—.

MRS. NORTON is very grateful to Mrs. Grantly for her kind present. The flowers are indeed beautiful and the grapes most delicious; she begs to send her best thanks for this thoughtful attention. She fears that there is but a very remote prospect of her being restored to health, but she is equally obliged to Mrs. Grantly for her good wishes.

LAUREL VILLA, STEPNEY.

To a Lady, after a First Visit at her House.

18, PERTH TERRACE, W.,
September 24th, 18—.

MY DEAR MRS. SOMERS,

I must tell you how very much we enjoyed our little visit to you last week, and the charming drives and walks we had; my husband says he does not know when he has spent a pleasanter week, he is so fond of the country and country amusements, and I assure you we both thoroughly appreciated all your hospitality and kindness. I had heard so much of your place and was quite anxious to see it; it really is one of the prettiest places I have ever seen, and how perfect you have made the house, I call it a triumph of good taste. We are going into Warwickshire in October to pay a few visits, but we shall be in town again early in November and remain there for the whole of the winter, and I hope if you think of coming up before Christmas you will let me know.

Remember me kindly to Mr. Somers, and believe me,
Very sincerely yours,
AMY B. CLAY.

CHAPTER VI.

PROPOSALS OF MARRIAGE.

From a Gentleman to a Lady to whom he has not been Introduced.

6, BEACH TERRACE, BRIGHTON,
May 26th, 18—.

DEAR MISS BARCOMBE,

I am aware that I am taking a very unusual step in venturing to address you, but I trust under the circumstances you will be inclined to excuse it, as unfortunately there appears to be no other course open to me of making myself known to you. Your beauty, dear Miss Barcombe, has inspired me with a sincere affection for yourself, and the various occasions on which I have had the pleasure of seeing you have served but to deepen the impression you at first created; and the one hope that animates me in thus writing to you, is that you may be induced to return my affection and ultimately become my wife. My position and means would, I think, be found satisfactory by your friends, and I trust you will give me an early opportunity of pleading my suit in person, and of offering every possible explanation to your relatives respecting my prospects in life. In the meantime I should tell you that I have lately become a junior partner in the firm of Messrs. Lewes and Lewes, civil engineers, and that I am thoroughly able to maintain a wife in comfort, if not in luxury. I venture to enclose my photograph. Dare I hope that it may mutely speak for me?

Believe me,
Dear Miss Barcombe,
Very truly yours,
CLAUDE LAWRANCE.

From a Gentleman to a Lady unaware of his Matrimonial Intentions.

102, CLEVELAND SQUARE, W.,
January 21st, 18—.

MY DEAR MISS CLARKE,

Although I have met you very frequently at your father's house and elsewhere, and although your manner has been most kind and friendly towards me, I dare not flatter myself that you are aware of the sincere affection I entertain for you, an affection which now emboldens me to write to you, and to tell you that the hope of gaining your love and of inducing you to become my wife, has been for the last few months uppermost in my mind. Should I be so fortunate as to win your regard and love, your happiness should be my one thought and care, and you should never regret having entrusted it to my keeping.

I shall await your answer with the greatest impatience. If you can give me hope, hasten to put an end to my doubts, and make me the happiest of men.

If, on the other hand, you require time for consideration, do not be afraid to ask me for it. Now that you know how dearly I love you I can afford to leave my cause in your hands, and to wait any length of time you may consider necessary for your final decision.

Believe me, dear Miss Clarke,
Yours very faithfully,
HENRY HART.

From a Gentleman to a Lady to whom he has been paying Attentions.

THE HERMITAGE, SAFFRON WALDEN,
July 25th, 18—.

MY DEAR MISS WILLIAMS,

I hope I am not mistaken in thinking that you are aware of the nature of the sentiments I entertain for you ; I trust I have made this very plain in the attentions I have had the happiness of paying you, but lest any doubt should exist in your mind as to the strength of my attachment let me tell you how very dear you are to me, and how each time I have seen you the feeling has deepened into more ᵔ ᵔted love.

ᵔl sure that I am not indifferent to you, and that were

it otherwise, you are too good to have misled me into believing this, and therefore I do not hesitate to ask for your love. May I write to your father on this subject at once? you see I take your consent for granted. Still, my dearest, I shall look with some anxiety for the assurance that I have not misunderstood your feelings, and that you return my affection, and that before long I may have the happiness of claiming you as my wife.

Believe me ever yours
Devotedly,
FREDERICK CHALLIS.

From a Gentleman to a Lady on having seen her but Twice.

5, RADSTOCK GARDENS, W.,
June 18*th*, 18—.

MY DEAR MISS ARMITAGE,

I am afraid you will accuse me of acting upon impulse only, from my venturing to write to you on so short an acquaintance, but were I to wait for months it would make no difference in my feelings towards you. I have met you, it is true, but twice, and my declaration of affection may perhaps appear precipitate in your eyes, but will you not make allowances for this in consideration of the true and lasting feeling of regard with which you have inspired me? I am convinced I shall never love anyone but you, and all I ask at present is to be allowed the opportunity of endeavouring to gain your affection, and of being received by yourself and family as a suitor for your hand. I trust you will not refuse me this much, as the happiness of my life, I feel, depends upon my success in obtaining your consent to become my wife at no distant day.

I do not anticipate any objections on the part of your father as far as my position and income are concerned, at least I think he will consider them satisfactory.

Hoping to have a favourable answer from you in the course of a day or two,

Believe me
Dear Miss Armitage,
Yours very truly,
GEORGE LOWTHER.

To a Lady, from a Gentleman who is Doubtful of being Accepted on account of his Small Means.

3, ROSEMONT VILLAS, BARNES,
May 15th, 18 —

DEAR MISS GRAY,

I have been pondering in my mind for some time whether it would be best to write to you or speak to you on the subject that is nearest to my heart, or whether it would be wiser for your sake to keep silence altogether; however, I have now decided to write to you and plead my cause as best I can.

Do you think you could be happy as the wife of a poor man? would you be content to wait until such time as my income would justify me in marrying? would the knowledge that my heart is all your own induce you to feel a corresponding affection for me? or am I asking too much? Would you be afraid to enter into a long engagement, an engagement of perhaps two years? Although I am not in a position to maintain a wife at the present moment, my prospects are encouraging, and I have a promise of being taken into partnership in my uncle's firm early in next year, which will materially improve my position. In the meantime the knowledge that I am working for you will brighten every hour of my life, while for your goodness in thus waiting and trusting, no after-devotion on my part can ever repay.

I hope your answer will not be long delayed, as I shall be all impatience to receive it.

Believe me, dear Miss Gray,
Yours very faithfully,
JOHN REDGRAVE.

From a Gentleman of Middle Age to a Young Lady.

FERN LODGE, WIMBLEDON,
July 4th, 18—.

DEAR MISS PALMER,

I have had the pleasure of meeting you very frequently lately at the houses of our mutual friends, and each occasion has served to strengthen the impression made upon me on first seeing you. I should consider myself the most fortunate of men if I could persuade you to accept me as your future husband. I am well aware of the disparity of age that exists between us, but I trust this will not be a

bar to my happiness, and that you will not regard it as such.
I am still, I flatter myself, in the prime of life, and the experience my years give me will better enable me to shiesd
your youth, and be protector and considerate counsellor, al
well as the most devoted of husbands, if you will give me
the right to be so.

Although I am not a rich man by any means, still I can
offer you every possible comfort that easy circumstances
admit of. As to my position and surroundings, they are, I
believe, well known to you. I have only to add that I trust
I have not been premature in disclosing my hopes, and that
they may receive favourable consideration at your hands.

Pray believe me, dear Miss Palmer,
Very faithfully yours,
CHARLES WOOD.

From a Widower to a Young Lady.

6, WARRIOR SQUARE, ST. LEONARDS,
September 2nd, 18—.

MY DEAR MISS FIELDING,

I am about to ask you a very serious question which
nearly concerns my happiness, and I trust you will be able
to return me a favourable answer. From what I have seen
of your amiable disposition and gentleness, I feel sure that
you would make me a sweet and loving wife and companion.
Will you consent to this, and be the mother of my darling
children? They are so young that at present they have
hardly recognised their loss. They have already learned to
love you, and it is in your power to fill up the void that
now exists both in my heart and home.

It is now two years since I suffered a loss which I then
thought irreparable, but since I have known you, I have
felt that there was yet happiness in store for me, if you
would accept the love I have to offer you, none the less
sincere because I have loved before, and have mourned so
deeply. Do not hesitate to tell me frankly whether the
interest I have awakened in your heart is a feeling of regard for myself or merely one of compassion for my lonely
condition. One word as regards my circumstances. I
have a fairly good income, but this is a matter for your
father's consideration, and I know that I can satisfy him on
this point.

Shall I call and receive your answer to-morrow from

yourself, or will you write to me? Perhaps the latter would be best.

Believe me, dear Miss Fielding,
Yours very faithfully,
ROBERT MANNERS.

Proposal from a Widower with grown-up Daughters to a Young Lady.

HEATH LODGE, NORWOOD,
July 22nd, 18—.

DEAR MISS LINDSAY,

I think you must be aware what pleasure I take in your society, how greatly I have been fascinated by your many attractions, and how much I admire all your amiable qualities. I fear I am only one of the many who have already told you this, but still I venture to hope that I am not altogether indifferent to you. Your friends will perhaps tell you that I am old enough to be your father, and that a man with grown-up daughters ought not to think of making so young a girl his wife, but in spite of my being well over forty, my sympathies and affections are as keen as if I were twenty years younger, and if you will accept me, it shall be the study of my life to make you happy. You would be a sister and companion to my girls, and to myself the most beloved of wives. I will not press you to give me an answer at once; take time to consider if you think it would be for your happiness to link your fate with mine. I will only add how grateful I should be to you if you decide in my favour, and believe me,

Very faithfully yours,
EDWARD CHURCHILL.

From a Widower to a Widow.

GROVE HOUSE, CHELTENHAM,
March 7th, 18—.

MY DEAR MRS. READE,

Since I have known you and enjoyed the pleasure of your agreeable society, the loneliness of my lot has seemed to me more unendurable than heretofore, and your charming companionship has led me into thinking how much brighter my existence would be if I could persuade you that we should both be the happier, were we to unite in cheering each other's daily path, and thus lighten the burden of our mutual cares and responsibilities. You have the interest of your children very much at heart as I well know, and I am not less solicitous respecting the welfare of my motherless girls. I feel you would be a loving mother to them, and you might trust me to prove an affectionate and indulgent father to your high-spirited boys.

You and I have both had our griefs, but we are still too young to spend the remainder of our lives in regretting the past. I for my part will do all in my power to render your life happy and prosperous, and to shield you, as far as may be, from trouble and anxiety, if you will only give me the right to do so.

Hoping to receive an answer from you in accordance with these my most earnest wishes,

Believe me,
Very faithfully yours,
CHARLES LITTON.

From a Gentleman to a Wealthy Widow.

78, SILLWOOD STREET, BRIGHTON,
November 8th, 18—.

MY DEAR MRS. MONCK,

To say that I have long admired you would be to tell you what you already know, but hitherto I have felt a reluctance to express the warm feelings of regard I entertain for you, lest you should accuse me of mercenary motives, owing to the difference that exists in our fortunes, you having wealth at your command, and it being an acknowledged fact that I am a poor man. Your manner of late has been so kind—dare I say encouraging?—that it seems to me that I should be wronging your generous nature, if I allowed any false pride on my part to stand between me and my hopes. If I thought otherwise I should not be writing to you this morning. Dear Mrs. Monck, will you accept the devotion of my life, and let it be my one aim to make you happy? If sincere affection can do this, it is yours to command.

I shall see you this evening, let me have one line if possible before then.

Always faithfully yours,
ERNEST TEMPLE.

From a Gentleman to an Heiress.

6, CROMWELL PLACE, W.,
September 4th, 13—.

DEAR MISS GROVE,

Since I have had the happiness of knowing you, the one wish of my heart has been to become worthy of you, and to succeed in winning your affections. I know that you have many admirers, but none, I am sure, more devoted to you than myself. I have, I fear, the drawback in the eyes of your friends of being poor, and they may endeavour to make you believe that it is the heiress I love, but do not think so badly of me, dear Miss Grove, as to entertain so cruel a suspicion of one who, if you were penniless, would be proud to prove his devotion to you; but it is idle to distress you and myself with such doubts, let me rather assure you of the unchanging love I feel for you, and how confident I am that, with youth and hope in my favour, I have a bright career opening before me. I should be content to wait any time for the fulfilment of my wishes, that you and your friends might consider expedient, provided I had the knowledge that you returned my affection, and would lighten my probation by your sympathy and encouragement.

I have but inadequately expressed all that I would say, but you will, I am sure, take the will for the deed, and give me credit for all I have left unsaid.

With sincere regards,
Believe me,
Yours very truly,
HERBERT SUTTON.

From a Gentleman asking a Father for his Daughter's Hand.

10, PARK PLACE, LIVERPOOL,
February 1st, 18—.

DEAR SIR,

I venture to write to you upon a matter in which the happiness of my life is concerned. I have long admired your second daughter, Miss Louisa Longfield, and I trust I am not mistaken in thinking that she is not indifferent to me; indeed, I am confident that had I your permission to do so I could succeed in winning her affections, but I hesitate to say a word to her on this subject until assured that I have your sanction to address her. I have even delayed asking for your consent to be accepted as a suitor for your daughter's hand, fearing that you might consider my prospects hardly justify me in taking such a step, but I feel I can wait no longer to declare my sentiments, and to learn what chance there may be for me.

My salary and income together do not amount to more than £250 per annum, but with what you may be inclined to give your daughter should her marriage meet with your approval, I have no doubt that with prudence and economy I might be able to make a comfortable home for her.

Hoping you will give this letter your favourable consideration,

I remain, dear Sir,
Very faithfully yours,
WILLIAM ARMSTRONG.

To H. LONGFIELD, ESQ.

From a Gentleman to the Father of a Young Lady, soliciting his Consent.

6, ALBERT TERRACE, W.,
June 8th, 18—.

DEAR SIR,

I have been fortunate enough to gain your daughter's affections, and having spoken to her on the subject of my hopes yesterday, I hasten to ask for your consent to our engagement, trusting earnestly that you will not withhold it. It would be my constant endeavour to do all in my power to make her happy, and to prove that I was worthy of her choice. Before saying a word to her I talked the matter over with my father, and he has promised to do all he can to further my wishes, and says he will allow me £200 a year from October next, in addition to the salary I now receive. Your daughter fully understands my position, and is quite willing to accept the home I can offer her subject to your approbation.

I remain, dear Sir,
Faithfully yours,
ALFRED KING.

To EDWARD LYON, ESQ.

Proposal of Marriage to a Young Lady from a Gentleman previously Rejected.

THE CEDARS, TOOTING,
July 15th, 18—.

MY DEAR MISS WHITE,

You will perhaps think me very foolish in again putting a question to you which you answered so discouragingly a year ago; but I have a faint hope that I may not now receive the same answer, and that time has done something in my favour. I cannot help trusting that my unchanging devotion to yourself has awakened some corresponding feeling of regard for me in your heart; I incline to this belief from little indications in your manner which I fancy I have observed, slight in themselves, but still sufficiently marked to embolden me to write to you. If I am mistaken, forgive me for urging my suit anew, and believe me always,

Yours very truly,
FRANCIS NAPIER.

From a Gentleman, soliciting his Father's Consent to his Engagement.

ROME,
January 17th, 18—.

MY DEAR FATHER,

I am afraid you will hardly be pleased at the purport of this letter. I write to ask your consent to my marriage with Miss Claremont; I anticipate all your objections, but I hope your affection for me will induce you to waive them, and that my dear mother will use all her influence with you in my behalf. I need not tell you how good and amiable and charming Miss Claremont is; you have only to know her to appreciate her many loveable qualities. She will make the best of wives, and I only want your and my dear mother's consent to make me the happiest of men.

Believe me, my dear father,
Your affectionate son,
HERBERT COOPER.

From a Lady to her Guardian, soliciting his Consent to her Engagement.

8, BEECH TERRACE, BOURNEMOUTH,
July 3rd, 18—.

DEAR MR. BRUCE,

Since I last wrote to you I have received a proposal of marriage from Mr. Edward Gray, with whom I think you are slightly acquainted. He is very much attached to me, and I have a great esteem and regard for him; so much so, that I have told him I would endeavour to obtain your consent to our engagement, and I trust you will see no reason for withholding it. Mr. Gray says he would be very pleased to explain his position and prospects fully to you if you will allow him the opportunity, and he trusts that you will find both satisfactory. I thoroughly understand the importance of the step I wish to take, but as my future happiness is deeply concerned in this matter, I hope you will return a favourable answer to our mutual wishes.

With all kind regards, believe me,
Dear Mr. Bruce,
Very sincerely yours,
GERTRUDE OSBORNE.

From a Father to a Gentleman, forbidding him to Pay his Addresses to his Daughter.

GRANVILLE PLACE, GUILDFORD,
May 7th, 18—.

DEAR SIR,

Your attentions to my daughter have become so marked of late, that I must beg you to discontinue them. I do not approve of you as a suitor for my daughter's hand, simply on the ground of your want of means; and I consider that you have not been acting fairly towards her in endeavouring to gain her affections, not being in a position to make a home for her. I have my daughter's promise that she will neither write to you or see you without my consent, and I rely upon your honour to respect my wishes, and not to attempt any further communication with her.

I am,
Dear Sir,
Yours faithfully,
GEORGE HAYWOOD.

F

From the Father of a Young Lady to the Father of a Young Gentleman, disapproving of his Son's Attentions to his Daughter.

THE CHESTNUTS, TEDDINGTON,
June 24th, 18—.

DEAR SIR,

I am sorry to have to write to you on a somewhat delicate subject; the fact is, your son has been paying my daughter considerably more attention than I think desirable, and a word from you would no doubt put a stop to anything further. He has been on such a friendly footing with my family that I did not apprehend that anything like a serious attachment was likely to spring up between your son and either of my daughters; however, from what I gather, such is the case.

I am sure you will agree with me that a marriage between my daughter Agnes and your boy would be most imprudent, if not altogether impossible. I take for granted that he cannot look to you for an allowance upon which to support a wife, while I am certainly not in a position to do anything for my daughter; under these circumstances, perhaps the best thing would be for the young people to discontinue meeting for the present.

Were your son of age I should take a different line with him; as it is, I leave it to you to bring him to reason; should he be so foolish as to persist I shall take care that my daughter understands that she is not to encourage him in his attentions.

I am,
Dear sir,
Yours faithfully,
W. HAWKINS.

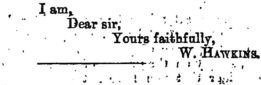

From the Father of a Young Lady to a Gentleman, requesting to know his Intentions.

MEADOW BANK, SUNBURY,
April 27th, 18—.

DEAR SIR,

I consider it my duty to ask you frankly what are your intentions towards my daughter. She is evidently very much attached to you, and your attentions to her have awakened a deep interest in her loving and affectionate heart. She has been too well brought up to think of bestowing her love where it was not desired, and I cannot allow her happiness to be trifled with. I therefore hope that you will see the propriety of at once putting an end to a position embarrassing to her as it is painful to me.

Awaiting your answer,

I am, dear Sir,

Yours very faithfully,

ROBERT CANNON.

To HORACE FARMER, Esq.

CHAPTER VII.

ANSWERS TO PROPOSALS OF MARRIAGE.

From a Lady to a Gentleman to whom she has not been Introduced, declining a Proposal of Marriage.

May 27th, 18—.

MISS BARCOMBE was naturally very much surprised at the contents of Mr. Lawrence's letter. She hastens to inform him that it is out of the question she can entertain his proposals. She need not trouble him with her reasons for this decision, beyond saying that they are quite conclusive, and she very much regrets, for Mr. Lawrence's sake, that he should have allowed himself to think of her for a moment. She begs to return his photo, and to add that she trusts the impression she appears to have made upon him will prove but a very transitory one.

10, SYDNEY PLACE, BRIGHTON.

Favourable answer from a Lady to a Gentleman to whom she has not been Introduced.

10, SYDNEY PLACE, BRIGHTON,
May 27th, 18—.

DEAR SIR,

Your letter received this morning surprised me not a little, coming from one who is an entire stranger to me. I at once showed it to my aunt, with whom I am staying, and she considers it so straightforward, that she sees no objection to your calling on her, especially as she is slightly acquainted with some members of your family. My aunt will be at home about four o'clock, but you must not consider this permission to call as an encouragement of your hopes on my part. It is merely an opportunity afforded by my aunt of our becoming acquainted.

Believe me,
Very truly yours,
HELEN BARCOMBE.

Favourable answer from a Lady respecting a Proposal of Marriage.

5, TAVISTOCK GARDENS, S.W.,
April 26th, 18—.

DEAR MR. HART,

I have hitherto looked upon you only as a friend, and I can hardly yet realise that you wish me to regard you in any other light. From what I already know of you I have no doubt that you would make anyone very happy whom you loved, but although I have a great liking and esteem for you, I cannot, I fear, say that I return your affection or that I care for you as you deserve.

However, as I know how good and kind you are, and how highly both my father and mother think of you, I hope that in time I may learn to love you. I cannot say more at present. Please believe that I feel very grateful to you for the offer of your love, and remain,

Very sincerely yours,
LUCY CLARKE.

Unfavourable answer from a Lady respecting a Proposal of Marriage.

5, TAVISTOCK GARDENS, S.W.,
April 26th, 18—.

DEAR MR. HART,

Your letter has occasioned me much pain, because I feel I have but one answer to make to it. I wish for your sake it were otherwise, but you must only think of me as a friend.

Greatly as I appreciate the honour you have done me in asking me to become your wife, I still feel that I must hold out no hope to you of such a possibility. I beg you will accept this answer as final, and not press me for a reason. I shall always value your friendship very highly, and I trust that after a little time we may meet again as friends, and that you will forgive me for the disappointment of to-day, which I have so unwillingly caused you.

With best wishes for your happiness,
Believe me yours,
,Very sincerely,
LUCY CLARKE.

Favourable answer from a Lady to a Gentleman whose Attentions have been agreeable to Her.

6, CLARENCE TERRACE, S.W.,
July 27th, 18—.

DEAR Mr. CHALLIS,

Your letter has made me very happy. I have often thought from your manner to me that you cared for me; how could I think otherwise, from the way in which you constantly devoted yourself to me? Still I was very glad to receive the confession of your sincere attachment, and I will not attempt to conceal how truly I return it, and how earnestly I trust I may prove worthy of it. I feel sure, that there is perfect sympathy between us, and that my happiness will be as safe in your hands as yours will be in mine.

I have told my father of your proposal, and he wishes me to say, that he will be pleased to hear from you.

Believe me yours,
Always affectionately,
BEATRICE WILLIAMS.

Favourable answer from a Lady to a Proposal from a Gentleman whom she has seen but Twice.

26, CLIFFORD SQUARE, W.,
June 20th, 18—.

DEAR MR. LOWTHER,

Your letter is a very difficult one to answer. I cannot but feel flattered at the admiration you express, and grateful for the affection you apparently feel for me. My being able to return it is of course a matter for future consideration, and you must not blame me should I fail in so doing.

My mother is of opinion that there is no reason why you should not be received at our house on the footing you desire, and for my part I shall be much pleased to see you.

Believe me,
Very sincerely yours,
ETHEL ARMITAGE.

Unfavourable answer from a Lady to a Proposal from a Gentleman whom she has seen but Twice.

MISS ARMITAGE begs to thank Mr. Lowther for his letter, and for the high opinion he has formed of her, but although sensible of the honour he has done her she regrets to say it is quite out of her power to receive him on the footing he suggests, or to hold out the hope that she can ever be anything to him beyond an acquaintance. Circumstances into which she need not enter preclude her coming to any other decision; and she trusts Mr. Lowther will not be offended at her frankness, and will not allow himself to think of her any further.

26, CLIFFORD SQUARE, W.,
    June 20th, 18—,

Favourable answer from a Lady to a Gentleman respecting a Long Engagement.

THE FIRS, PUTNEY,
    May 17th, 18—.

DEAR MR. REDGRAVE,

I will not say your letter was unexpected or that I am surprised at its contents; on the contrary I almost knew beforehand what you were anxious to say to me and what I was anxious to hear; you cannot suppose I should be afraid to be a poor man's wife; my love would be little worth having if I were : no, I do not dread a long engagement, it will give us time to know each other better; my attachment to you is sufficiently strong to bear the strain. I am not afraid that your feelings will undergo a change towards me or that mine will alter towards you. Indeed should either of us cease to love the other it would only prove how wise we were to put our affection to the test by waiting.

My mother, I am sorry to say, entertains a prejudice against a long engagement; she has no real objection to it, however, and has a personal liking for you, so I think she will not oppose it as she will know that my happiness is so deeply concerned, and together I hope we shall make her believe that she approves of our attachment and of our engagement.

I shall hope to see you to-morrow; dear Mr. Redgrave,

Believe me,
            Yours lovingly,
                EVELYN GRAY.

Unfavourable answer from a Lady to a Gentleman respecting a Long Engagement.

THE FIRS, PUTNEY,
May 17th, 18—.

DEAR MR. REDGRAVE,

I am deeply grieved at the answer I am obliged to give you ; but, believe me, I have no alternative than to write as ˙I am now doing. My father will not for a moment hear of our engagement, and whatever my own feelings may be you would not, I am sure, wish me to disobey him. He considers a long engagement would be most imprudent on our part; he says you may not be in the same mind two years hence, and that your prospects are too uncertain to render such a step advisable.

All this sounds cold and hard ; but coming from him it must be said. I dare not hold out a hope that if we are both free " two years hence," you might expect a very different answer, because this might appear in the light of a secret understanding, and would be obeying my father in the letter but not in the spirit, which would naturally pain him very much. Still I do not think that I shall easily forget you, or cease to think of you, or cease to take a warm interest in all that concerns you. Dear Mr. Redgrave, goodbye, forgive me for the disappointment I am compelled to inflict upon you, think of me kindly, and believe me

Yours very sincerely,
EVELYN GRAY.

Favourable answer from a Young Lady to a Middle-aged Gentleman respecting a Proposal of Marriage.

THE ELMS, TWICKENHAM,
July 6th, 18—.

DEAR MR. WOOD,

I very much appreciate the honour you have done me in asking me to marry you ; although I have a great esteem and regard for you, I have not hitherto thought of you as a lover, but perhaps in time I may feel for you the affection which is due from a woman to the ˉone who is to be her husband, only you must be content to wait a little, and not expect too much from me just at first. I may tell you that my heart is quite disengaged, and that you have no rival to contend with, merely the ideal hero who finds a place in the imagination of most girls. My sister thinks that I am very fortunate to have won your affections, and she hopes that you will soon give her an opportunity of telling you so. I shall remain with her for the next three weeks, when mamma is coming up for a few days. I have written to tell her of your letter, and shall doubtless hear from her.

With my sister's kind regards and mine, believe me, dear Mr. Wood,

Very sincerely yours,
EDITH PALMER.

Unfavourable answer from a Young Lady to a Middle-aged Gentleman respecting a Proposal of Marriage.

THE ELMS, TWICKENHAM,
July 6th, 18—.

DEAR MR. WOOD,

While thanking you very much for the high compliment you have paid me in asking me to be your wife, I cannot, I regret to say, entertain your proposals. I like you very much indeed as a friend, but I am quite sure I should not be happy with one so much older than myself. You would probably think me foolish if not frivolous, and I should very likely fear you more than I should love you. I am convinced I should not be a suitable wife for you—please do not think of me in that light, as it would not be for the happiness of either of us.

My sister thinks otherwise, and would have me return a very different answer; but you are too good and kind for anyone to marry you save from motives of affection.

With all good wishes, believe me,

Very sincerely yours,
EDITH PALMER.

Favourable answer from a Young Lady to a Widower respecting a Proposal of Marriage.

BELMONT, ST. LEONARDS,
Sept. 3rd, 18—.

DEAR MR. MANNERS,

You are quite right in thinking that I have been very much interested in you and in your sweet children. I have felt so sorry for you and for them. Do you really think I could be to you all you say and replace her whom you have lost? I should not be afraid to undertake the responsibility of being a mother to your little pets, if I were certain it would be for your happiness; mine I am sure would be secured by a union with you, and I do not know why I should hesitate to tell you that I will be to you everything you wish. I have not said anything to my father at present. I would rather leave it to you to do so; he has so great a regard for you, that I know you will be well received by him.

Believe me, dear Mr. Manners,
Yours very sincerely,
SYBIL FIELDING.

Unfavourable answer from a Young Lady to a Widower respecting a Proposal of Marriage.

BELMONT, ST. LEONARDS,
Sept. 3rd, 18—.

DEAR MR. MANNERS,

I very much regret that the friendly interest I have taken in you and in your dear little children, should have led you to imagine that I entertained any warmer feeling towards you than that of friendship; perhaps it would be kinder to tell you at once that my affections are already engaged, although there is no immediate prospect of my marriage, and our engagement is at present only known to the members of my family. My heart being devoted to another, I felt at liberty to evince an almost sisterly liking for you, in my endeavour to cheer you and lighten your sorrow. I am deeply grieved to have unintentionally misled you into thinking I cared for you in the way you wish.

Now that you know the reason why I cannot return your affection, you will not, I trust, think I am to blame, and allow me to regard you as one of my greatest friends.

Pray believe me, dear Mr. Manners, with kindest wishes for your happiness,

Yours very truly,
SYBIL FIELDING.

Favourable answer from a Young Lady to a Widower with grown-up Daughters, respecting a Proposal of Marriage.

THE LIMES, SYDENHAM,
July 25th, 18—.

DEAR MR. CHURCHILL,

I have taken time to consider the contents of your kind letter, that I might be quite sure I was making a wise decision. It is not the difference of age between us that has made me a little doubtful as to how I should answer you, but rather as to how I should be received in your family, and whether my coming amongst you in this new position would not make things unpleasant for you as well as for myself. Your daughters are great friends of mine, it is true, but would they not feel aggrieved at my being the mistress of a house over which they have themselves had solo control. However, I am perhaps too sensitive in this matter, and I should be wrong to sacrifice your happiness and my own to an idea which perhaps is unfounded. I have said enough for you to understand the feelings with which I regard you, and if after reading this letter you still think I should make you happy, I will offer no further objection to your wishes.

Believe me, dear Mr. Churchill,
Very truly yours,
MAUD LINDSAY.

Unfavourable answer from a Young Lady to a Widower with grown-up Daughters respecting a Proposal of Marriage.

THE LIMES, SYDENHAM,
July 25th, 18—.

DEAR MR. CHURCHILL,

Much as I like and esteem you, I nevertheless shrink from the responsibility of the position you offer me. I do not think such a step would be either for your happiness or for mine. Your daughters would very naturally regard me as an intruder, and would feel very pained at your marrying a girl as young as themselves. I am quite serious in what I say and am not the least likely to think differently ; I therefore hope you will soon view my decision in the same light as I do, that is to say, as the only fitting one under the circumstances.

With all good wishes,
Yours very truly,
MAUD LINDSAY.

Favourable answer from a Widow to a Widower.

5, PARK CRESCENT, CHELTENHAM,
March 9th, 18 —.

DEAR MR. LITTON,
Your straightforward letter merits an equally candid reply. I too have realised the loneliness of my position very forcibly, and your kindly interest in me has led me insensibly to depend upon you for advice and counsel in every little difficulty, while your friendship has been a source of great comfort to me. I entertain a very high opinion of your character, and feel sure that my future and that of my children would be safe in your hands, and I think I may frankly accept a proposal made in such evident good faith, especially as I can promise to be to you a considerate and devoted wife and friend.

I remain, yours very truly,
SOPHIA READE.

Unfavourable answer from a Widow to a Widower.

5, PARK CRESCENT, CHELTENHAM,
March 9th, 18—.

DEAR MR. LITTON,
Highly as I value your friendship, I cannot, I regret to say, entertain any warmer feeling for you. I fully appreciate the compliment you have paid me in asking me to marry you, but I do not think such a step would be for my happiness. I have no doubt you would be all you say both to me and to my children, but yet I must decline your offer, much as it pains me to disappoint you. I trust in giving you this answer I shall not lose a friend whom I greatly esteem, and, with kind regards and good wishes, believe me,

Yours very truly,
SOPHIA READE.

Favourable answer from a wealthy Widow to a Gentleman.

29, SUSSEX CRESCENT, BRIGHTON,
November 8th, 18—.

DEAR MR. TEMPLE,

How very foolish of you to be so unjust to yourself and to me as to fancy I could for a moment believe you capable of unworthy motives or that you would feign a love you did not feel. I have too high an opinion of you and of your principles to be otherwise than flattered by your preference. After your frank confession of regard for me, I will not hesitate to say that I feel well inclined towards you, so well indeed, that I think I may bid you hope; you must not be too impatient, but give me time to be certain that in marrying you I should be consulting my own happiness as well as yours. I cannot say more at present, and remain,

Yours very sincerely,
CHARLOTTE MONCK.

Unfavourable answer from a wealthy Widow to a Gentleman.

29, SUSSEX CRESCENT, BRIGHTON,
November 8th, 18—.

DEAR MR. TEMPLE,

I do not, I assure you, suspect that your professions of affection for myself are dictated from mercenary motives, and while declining your proposal I do full justice to your high principles, but I have no other feeling for you than that of mere friendship, and if anything in my manner has led you to think otherwise, I can only say that I regret it, and that it was quite unintentional on my part.

I remain, dear Mr. Temple,
Very truly yours,
CHARLOTTE MONCK.

Favourable answer from an Heiress, to a Gentleman.

HERMITAGE PARK, WIMBLEDON,
September 6th, 18—.

DEAR MR. SUTTON,

Your letter made me at once happy and unhappy; happy in knowing that you love me, and unhappy at the opposition which I fear awaits us both at the hands of my uncle and guardian. It will be very difficult to make him believe in your disinterested affection, and even more so to gain his consent to our engagement; from the few words he said to me on the subject I know he holds very strong opinions against my marrying any one who has not some means of his own. I need not tell you that I do not share this idea, I am only glad that I am rich for your sake, but we must both be brave, and trust in the future. You must not take umbrage at anything my uncle may say to you, and I will endeavour to make amends for any harshness on his part you may have to endure, by showing you how much I value your love.

With kindest wishes, but with rather a sinking heart,

I remain,

Yours affectionately,

ISABELLE GROVE.

_____

Unfavourable answer from an Heiress, to a Gentleman.

HERMITAGE PARK, WIMBLEDON,
September 6th, 18—.

DEAR MR. SUTTON,

I am much flattered by the favourable impression I appear to have made upon you, but I have not thought of you as a possible husband, although as an agreeable partner at a ball I liked you very much, but to speak frankly I am certain I should never care for you save as an acquaintance. I am afraid, in spite of your disclaimer to the contrary, that were it not for the accident of my heiressship, you would not have thought of proposing to me, but be this as it may it would not influence the answer I have to give you, and I think it is kindest and best to tell you at once, that there is no hope of my changing my mind or of my feeling differently towards you.

Thanking you for the honour you have done me, believe me, Sincerely yours,

ISABELLE GROVE.

_____

Favourable answer from the Father of a Young Lady to a Gentleman who has solicited her hand.

WOODSTOCK LODGE, LIVERPOOL,
Feb. 4th, 18—.

DEAR SIR,

I cannot say that I altogether approve of early marriages, or think it right that a young man should rely, upon other than his own resources when he contemplates maintaining a wife. However as my daughter's happiness is my first consideration, and as I find on questioning her that she is evidently attached to you, I shall not oppose your engagement, and I will do what I can to enable you to marry, but in justice to my other children I cannot promise to do much, and £100 a-year is the utmost allowance I can make her, and I shall further expect you both to wait at least six months which at your time of life ought to be and indeed is no hardship; any way this is the decision I have arrived at after mature deliberation.

I am, dear Sir,

Faithfully yours,

ROBERT LONGFIELD.

Unfavourable answer from the Father of a Young Lady, to a Gentleman who has solicited her hand.

WOODSTOCK LODGE, LIVERPOOL,
Feb. 4th, 18—.

DEAR SIR,

The only part of your letter which afforded me any satisfaction is that wherein you say you have not spoken to my daughter respecting your hopes. I may as well inform you that I am not prepared to make her any allowance on her marriage. What she will receive from me at my death is a question for my future consideration. I do not intend her to marry a man who cannot support her without coming to her father for help, and you will distinctly understand that I beg to decline your proposals for her hand.

I am, dear Sir,

Faithfully yours,

R. LONGFIELD.

Favourable answer from a Father, to a Gentleman soliciting his Consent.

THE BEECHES, CLAPHAM,
June 9th, 18—.

DEAR SIR,

Since my daughter's happiness is concerned in obtaining my consent to her engagement with you, I can only say that I will offer no opposition to it, and shall be glad to receive you at our house as her accepted lover. I trust that you will, as you say, make her a good husband.

I will endeavour to see your father in a day or two, and explain to him what I can afford to do for my daughter.

Faithfully yours,

EDWARD LYON.

Unfavourable answer from a Father, to a Gentleman soliciting his Consent.

THE BEECHES, CLAPHAM,
June 9th, 18—.

DEAR SIR,

It seems to me that you have been premature in speaking to my daughter as you have done, without previously learning my wishes on the subject. I am very much displeased with her for giving you any encouragement, as she fully understood that it would be contrary to my views were she to do so; however it obliges me to tell you distinctly that I decline to give my consent to any engagement between you, and I am not likely to alter this determination.

I am, Sir, yours faithfully,

E. LYON.

Unfavourable answer from a Lady to a Gentleman whom she has previously Rejected.

70, CUMBERLAND PLACE, REGENT'S PARK, W.,
July 17th, 18—.

DEAR MR. NAPIER,

I am indeed sorry to pain you by repeating the refusal I gave you a year ago; time has made no difference in my feelings towards you. I am grateful for the devotion you profess for me, and I only regret I cannot make you a better return, but I can offer you no further hope beyond saying that I shall always esteem you as a friend.

Yours very truly,

VIOLET WHITE.

Unfavourable answer from a Father to a Son, respecting his Engagement.

NIGHTINGALE LODGE, STREATHAM,
Jan. 28th, 18—.

MY DEAR HERBERT,

It is quite out of the question that I should countenance your engagement with Miss Claremont. I have no doubt that she is all you say, but I must remind you that you are not in a position to maintain a wife; you have your own way to make in the world, and have no right to suppose that I can allow you sufficient income to marry upon. I should be unjust to your brothers and sisters were I to do so; and I beg you to understand that you have nothing to expect from me if you persist in your imprudence, which I can only regard as a boyish infatuation. Your mother sends her love, and says she is sure you will not be so rash and foolish as to act contrary to my wishes.

Believe me, my dear boy,

Your affectionate father,

ALFRED COOPER.

Unfavourable answer from a Guardian to his Ward respecting her Engagement.

ST. MICHAEL'S, GLASGOW,

July 6th, 18—,

MY DEAR MISS OSBORNE,

I do not consider that Mr. Edward Gray would be a desirable husband for you in any way. I am sorry that you should have allowed matters to go as far as they have done, as I understand from your letter that you have partially accepted him. However, I have your interest too much at heart to give my consent to a marriage which I am convinced would not ultimately be for your happiness, and I am sure that you are possessed of too much good sense to act contrary to my opinion. In my responsible position as your guardian, I must advise you to the best of my judgment in what affects your welfare; and, disagreeable as it is to me to oppose your wishes, I feel it my duty to write to you as I am now doing.

If you desire it, I will myself communicate with Mr. Gray.

I remain, dear Miss Osborne,

Your sincere friend and guardian,

JAMES BRUCE.

From a Gentleman to the Father of a Young Lady who has forbidden him to pay his Addresses to his Daughter.

OAK LODGE, THAMES DITTON,
May 9th, 18—.

DEAR SIR,

Your letter occasioned me some surprise, as from the encouragement I have received to visit at your house and from the manner in which I have been allowed to devote myself to your daughter in public, at balls and parties and in society generally, I was under the impression that Mrs. Haywood and yourself tacitly approved of my attentions to her.

It would have been kinder had you thought proper to signify your disapproval six months ago, as my attentions must have been as patent to you as to every one else. However, as your daughter acquiesces in your views, I have nothing more to add beyond that I will respect your wishes, and beg to remain

Yours faithfully,
ARTHUR GREATHEAD.

From a Gentleman to the Father of a Young Lady, declaring that he has no Intentions towards his Daughter.

THE HERMITAGE, WALTON-ON-THAMES,
April 28th, 18—.

DEAR SIR,

I was very much surprised at the receipt of your letter, and I can only hope you are mistaken in supposing your daughter to be attached to me. I flatter myself that she regards me as a friend, and as such I have a sincere admiration and esteem for her; but you must excuse me if I say that I entertain no warmer feeling towards her, and that I have only paid her such attention as is due from a gentleman to a lady in whose society he is constantly thrown. Under these circumstances, I conclude you would wish me to discontinue my visits at your house. I shall do so with much regret, and with the kindest remembrance of the hospitality I have there received.

With compliments to Mrs. Cannon,
Believe me,
Very truly yours,
HORACE FARMER.

To ROBERT CANNON, Esq.

CHAPTER VIII.

LETTERS BETWEEN ENGAGED COUPLES RELATING TO IMPORTANT OCCASIONS.

From a Gentleman to a Lady on first being Accepted.

GROVE HOUSE, CHISLEHURST,
June 8th, 18—.

MY DEAR CLARA,

I have been awaiting your answer to my letter with the greatest impatience, and though you were too good to keep me long in suspense, still the interval between writing to you and hearing from you, was passed by me in alternate fear and hope—fear that I had mistaken your feelings, and hope that perhaps you did care for me a little. At present I can hardly realise the happiness of knowing that I may soon call you mine; it is the fulfilment of my dearest wishes.

Believe me, dearest, it will be my one thought and care to render your life a happy one as far as it lies in my power, and if we both love and trust each other we may, I hope, look forward to a bright future together. I was much gratified by your father's message to me, and I shall hope to run down to Ryde on Saturday next as he so kindly proposes. In the meantime, will you not send me a photo of yourself that I may show it to my mother, who is most anxious to know you, having heard from her son how sweet and loveable you are?

I remain, dearest Clara,
Your devoted
GILBERT FORSTER.

From a Gentleman to a Lady, to whom he has been recently engaged, during a first Temporary Absence.

GRAND HOTEL, PARIS,
May 18th, 18—.

MY DEAREST EVELYN,

You will be expecting to hear from me. I arrived here last night rather fatigued from a hurried journey and a rough crossing. I shall hope to find a letter from you on my arrival at the Hôtel de l'Europe, Lucerne. You may be sure I shall not remain away from you a day longer than is absolutely necessary to complete the business I have on hand, and you will, I am sure, give me the welcome I deserve for having made such haste to return to you. I picture you sitting under the chestnut-trees on the dear old lawn and, I trust, thinking of me. Excuse a short note to-day, I find it difficult to collect my thoughts. I leave this by the mid-day train.

Remember me to all your family; and believe me, dearest Evelyn,

Yours devotedly,
MAURICE FAIRFIELD.

A Lady's first Letter to a Gentleman to whom she is Engaged.

27, EARLSCOURT SQUARE, S.W.,
August 6th, 18—.

DEAREST FRANK,

You asked me to write you a long letter in answer to yours. It is a great happiness to me to do so, and to know that you care to hear all my thoughts, hopes, and wishes. I have read your letter again and again; the assurance it contains of your affection is very precious to me. Dear Frank, do you really love me as much as you say you do? I must not doubt it, but still it seems so strange and new to me that I should have the power of winning the heart of one so good and clever as you are, and that your choice should have fallen upon me. I am very proud it should be so; my heart is full of thoughts of you, and every hour of the day I look forward to being with you again. I try, oh so earnestly, to fit myself for the position that awaits me as your wife, that you may never

be disappointed in me, and that we may be all in all to
each other.
    With fondest love, believe me,
        Dearest Frank,
           Your affectionate and devoted
                      CECY.

**From a Gentleman to a Lady to whom he is Engaged,
asking her to name the Day of their Marriage.**

           COLWIN HOUSE, LIVERPOOL,
                December 2nd, 18—.
MY OWN DARLING,
    We have now- been engaged quite long enough to
understand each other thoroughly, and as far as I can see
there is no good reason for delaying our marriage. I have
not pressed you before on this point, but if you really love
me as I think you do, you will consent to make me happy
by naming an early day. Why should we not be married
immediately after Christmas? this would give you time for
any preparations you may have to make, while, as for myself, I should be quite ready to receive my dear little wife
next week, if she would only come to me. Dearest Annie,
will you consult your mother? I am sure she will say I am
right, in asking you not to put off our marriage any longer.
I cannot possibly get away from here for the next ten days
or so, but write and tell me it shall be as I wish.
    God bless you, darling.
           Your affectionate and devoted
                  ARTHUR CHESTER.

**From a Lady to a Gentleman to whom she is Engaged,
refusing to name an Early Day for the Marriage.**

        7, BRYANSTON TERRACE, W.,
                December 4th, 18—.
DEAREST ARTHUR,
    I wish I could write as you suggest, but there are
many reasons against our marriage taking place just at
present. We have as you say been engaged some little time,
but three months is, after all, a very short period in which
to learn the tastes, feelings, and ideas of one who is to be
life's dearest companion; besides which we have seen so
little of each other, and I cannot help feeling that this
period of our life is perhaps the sweetest and pleasantest
we may ever experience; married life will bring cares and

responsibilities with it, and I would prolong my present happiness, if I could. You must not be angry with me for saying this, dear Arthur, or for being rather reluctant to exchange happy certainty for the unknown future. My mother will not influence me either way, but allows me to judge for myself. She will be happy to see you here when you can arrange to come to us for a few days, and you and I can then talk things over, and perhaps your arguments may prove more convincing than mine, in which case I shall give way.

In the meantime I am, with love,
Your affectionate and attached

ANNIE LOWE.

From a Lady to a Gentleman to whom she is Engaged, naming the Day of their Marriage.

WARWICK HOUSE, LEAMINGTON,
November 23rd, 18—.

DEAREST HARRY,

Your dear letter made me very happy. You asked me a very momentous question, to name the day of our marriage. Dear Harry, it shall be as you wish; your arguments are so convincing I can only feel that you are right, and say yes to all you propose. My mother also thinks that the 20th of next month would not be too soon, and that I can make all my preparations within that time, therefore let it be the 20th. Our engagement seems all too brief, but I have such perfect trust in you, and we know each other so thoroughly, that I need not postpone our marriage with the idea of seeing more of you, and I feel I may look forward to our passing a very happy life together

Good-bye, dearest Harry; fondest love
From your own

AMY.

From a Lady to a Gentleman to whom she is Engaged, asking his Consent to the Postponement of their Marriage.

RADSTOCK HOUSE, SHAFTESBURY,
May 20th, 18—.

MY DEAR JAMES,

When I promised that our marriage should take place in July, I fully intended to keep my word, but on consideration I am determined to ask you to let it be

postponed for a few months longer. I have no good reason
to urge for this delay—perhaps I am over-sensitive and
anxious, but still if you would agree to it I should be very
grateful. I cannot help fearing we entered upon our
engagement rather hastily, and that I was persuaded
against my better judgment to fix July for our marriage.
I think it will be better for both our sakes that we should
endeavour to learn more of each other's tastes, and what
each requires of the other. Your line of life is so decided
that I wish to be certain I can fall in with it, or that you
would meet me in some degree with little concessions to my
individual tastes. I have written to you out of the fulness
of my heart, and I trust you will not misunderstand me,
or think I do not love you. I only ask for time, which I
am sure you will not refuse me.

Believe me, dear James,
Your ever affectionate
KATE CONWAY.

**From a Gentleman to a Lady to whom he is Engaged,
complaining of her Indifference.**

ROYAL HOTEL, SOUTHSEA,
August 18th, 18—.

DEAREST EDITH,
You must be aware that you are making me very
unhappy by the line of conduct you are pursuing. You
cannot suppose it is very pleasant to me to see you day
after day encouraging the attentions of other men. At the
ball last night you appeared to prefer every man in the
room to myself as a partner. If you acted in this way with
the idea of arousing my jealousy, let me tell you it is a very
dangerous game to play at; but I am afraid nothing so
flattering to myself was intended, and that a love of
admiration and indifference to my feelings were the
motives that actuated you. If this is the case, it would be
best for both of us that our engagement should be at an
end; if, however, you are able to assure me that you
meant nothing by your thoughtless coquetry beyond the
amusement of the moment, you shall never again hear a
word of reproach from me on this subject, and I will trust
you as fully as before.

Believe me, dearest,
Your ever faithful and affectionate
FREDERICK MARRIOT.

From a Gentleman to a Lady to whom he is Engaged, confessing his Jealousy.

ROYAL HOTEL, RYDE,
August 26th, 18—.

MY DEAR ROSE,

Is it your intention to break off your engagement with me ? I can only suppose it is so from the way you allow Mr. Little to devote himself to you. It seems everyone is aware he is paying you more attention than, under the circumstances, you ought to receive from any man save myself. Either he is ignorant of the engagement between us, or he is dishonourable enough to act in defiance of it. If you have not sufficient regard for my feelings and for your own position as my promised wife, to put an end at once to any further acquaintance with Mr. Little, you will understand that I resign all pretensions to your hand, but I should be sorry to think that you had changed so completely in the last few weeks as to care for me no longer. My sentiments have not altered towards you, in spite of all that has passed ; and it rests with you to say whether you prefer Mr. Little to myself. I shall of course abide by your decision, and remain,

Yours very truly,
HENRY BANKS.

From a Lady to a Gentleman to whom she is Engaged, complaining of his Coldness.

7, BOSCOWEN LODGE, MAIDA VALE,
August 10th, 18—.

MY DEAR EDWARD,

I have been trying to make up my mind for some time past to put my fears into words, but I have rather shrunk from doing so, hoping that perhaps I was mistaken ; but I can no longer delude myself into thinking this is the case. I feel you are very much changed, your manner to me at times almost amounts to indifference. Your letters are short and cold, and I cannot extract a word of affection from them. I am beginning to think you no longer care for me ; perhaps this is what you wish me to understand. And yet I can hardly believe this of you ; it must be that something or someone has estranged you from me, and that an explanation between us will put things on their former footing ; anyhow, I have given you the opportunity of telling me everything, and I implore you to be frank with me, as our future happiness depends upon our understanding each other.

> Believe me, dear Edward,
> Your affectionate
> MINNIE.

From a Lady to a Gentleman to whom she is Engaged, complaining of his Neglect.

> THE WILLOWS, UPPER NORWOOD,
> *June 21st,* 18—.

DEAREST RICHARD,

I have been expecting to hear from you for the last three weeks, and I cannot understand why you do not answer my letters. If I thought illness prevented your writing to me, I should be most unhappy about you, but I am glad to know that the contrary is the case. I am quite aware that you are fully occupied during the day, but still you used to find time for a letter two or three times a week. Has anything occurred to vex or annoy you? If so, will you not tell me what it is, and if it rests with me or with any of my family, perhaps I can explain it away. You know my father is always glad to see you—why have you kept away all this time? I have been so pained and wounded by your neglect; I have tried to make excuses to myself and to others; dear Richard, you should have written, if only a few lines; it appears so unkind to treat me with such a want of consideration.

> Believe me,
> Your affectionate and anxious
> KATE.

From the Mother of a Young Lady to her Daughter's Lover respecting a Quarrel.

> CLEVELAND PLACE, MORTLAKE,
> *April 6th,* 18—.

MY DEAR MR. NEWTON,

It is always a delicate matter for a third person to interfere in lovers' quarrels, but as the happiness of my child is at stake, I feel it my duty as her mother to try and bring about a reconciliation between you. I will not question which of you is in fault; all I wish is to see the smiles return to my child's face, and tranquillity to her heart. She is evidently very unhappy, but tries to conceal it

even from me. I think, dear Mr. Newton, that if you really love her, as I am sure you do, you will come to her on receipt of this letter, and you need have no fear of your reception. Trusting you will not misunderstand the feeling that actuates me in thus writing to you,
Believe me,
Very sincerely yours,
MARGARET LINDSAY.

From a Lady to a Gentleman to whom she is Engaged, and of whom she is Jealous.

7, HAMILTON TERRACE, REGENT'S PARK,
July 2nd, 18—.

MY DEAR ROBERT,

I hope you will not think me foolish or exacting if I say that I feel very pained and hurt at the attentions you so constantly offer to Miss Ward; I do not suppose you mean to vex me, and I have no doubt it is more her fault than yours, but still I wish you would be a little less *empressé* in your manner to her. You will think perhaps that I am jealous of her; it is not quite that, but yet I have a sort of feeling that I would rather you were not quite so nice to her. You will not be angry with me for saying this, dear Robert; it is my great love for you that causes me to attach such importance to every look and word of yours, and to feel reluctant that other women should share them with me. You must not say that this argues a want of trust in you unworthy of us both; indeed I do trust you, otherwise my self-respect would not allow me to write as frankly as I am now doing. I fancy I have only to tell you what is in my heart for you to give me no further cause for—shall I say jealousy? although I have tried to put this hateful word on one side.

Always, dear Robert,
Your loving
FLORENCE.

From a Gentleman to a Lady to whom he is Engaged, respecting her Jealousy of him.

17, POWIS TERRACE, N.W.,
July 3rd, 18—.

MY DEAR FLORENCE,

Your reproaches are entirely undeserved, and I am surprised at your permitting yourself to indulge in the feelings you have expressed. Much as I am attached to you, I must tell you, once for all, that I detest jealousy in a woman, and I should soon cease to care for one who tormented me by repetition of such accusations. If, during our engagement, you are to feel aggrieved at my offering the slightest civility to any lady of my acquaintance, what chance of happiness is there in store for us in married life? I can see nothing but unhappiness for both of us if you persist in giving way to this feeling; dismiss it from your mind, it is not worthy of you, and remember that perfect trust is what I expect and desire from her who is to become my wife. I feel strongly on this subject, as I have seen so much alienation and misery occasioned by unfounded jealousy.

Believe me, my dearest Florence,
Ever yours,
ROBERT GLOVER.

From a Gentleman to a Lady to whom he is Engaged, telling her she has no Cause for Jealousy.

6, GLOUCESTER GARDENS, N.W.,
July 3rd, 18—.

MY DEAREST FLORENCE,

It is certainly foolish of you to underrate your own attractions so far as to think I could prefer any one to yourself. Do not entertain such a thought for a moment. My heart is wholly yours, and I have not a thought to bestow upon any one else; and I did not in the least intend to convey anything beyond mere politeness by my attentions to Miss Ward; but if you think that I have inadvertently given you the least cause for uneasiness, you may depend upon my being very much on my guard in future, so as to avoid the faintest suspicion of a preference for the society of any young lady, save yourself, be she ever so charming.

Believe me, dearest Florence,
Ever yours,
EDWIN SIDNEY.

From a Gentleman to a Lady to whom he is Engaged, Apologising for Unfounded Jealousy.

THE GROVE, WIMBLEDON,
August 4th, 18—.

MY DEAREST FLORA,

I am quite satisfied, from the explanation you have given me, that my jealousy was unfounded, and I must ask for your forgiveness for having doubted you. I am afraid my accusations must have pained you very much, and I deeply regret having written as I did; but you are so good and gentle, I am sure you will receive me into favour on my promising never to offend again in a like manner. You must not be very angry with me for fearing to lose what I prize so dearly, the love of my darling Flora.

Once more, dearest, forgive me, and believe me
Your devoted
EDGAR BLAKE.

From a Lady to a Gentleman to whom she is Engaged, excusing herself for her Unwarrantable Jealousy.

BELLEVUE TERRACE, HARROGATE,
Sept. 9th, 18—.

MY DEAREST BASIL,

I have been so unhappy lately, thinking you did not care for me as you used to do, that the joy of receiving your letter, and learning that I still hold the first place in your heart, has been almost too much for me, and I have shed such happy tears. It is so hard to doubt one you love, and it seems that I have tormented myself quite unnecessarily all these past weeks; still you must admit I had some excuse for making myself miserable. What was I to think from your silence, and from all I heard? Dearest Basil, believe me, I will never doubt you again, never, never, and I shall always think you are the kindest, dearest, best, and truest of men, and that you are all my own.

I remain, now and always,
Your loving
AGGIE.

From a Lady to a Gentleman to whom she is Engaged,
breaking off her Engagement owing to Change of
Feeling towards him.

114, Russell Sq., W.,
February 17th, 18—.

Dear Hugh,

Believe me, I am sincerely grieved at the pain I fear
this letter will occasion you, and I trust you will not think
hardly of me for what I am about to say. I did not rightly
understand my own feelings when I accepted you, and
mistook esteem and friendship for love. Much as it costs
me to make this confession, I feel it is due to you, and
that I ought to tell you I can never entertain the affection
for you that you have a right to expect from your future
wife.

This knowledge has made me very unhappy, but I have
now determined to ask you to release me from my promise;
dear Hugh, forgive me; I venture to hope that some day
you will be as happy as you deserve, although it is not in
my power to make you so.

With kindest wishes,

Believe me,

Yours very sincerely,

Caroline Hardwick.

From a Lady to a Gentleman to whom she is Engaged,
breaking Off her Engagement on account of his
Indifference.

7, Connaught Terrace, Folkestone,
November 2nd, 18—.

Dear Mr. Lawrence,

You will doubtless not be surprised at the contents
of this letter, indeed you have hardly left me any alternative than to say that I wish our engagement to be at an
end. Perhaps I ought to have arrived at this decision
sooner, but I was reluctant to give you up until I felt quite
sure it was the right thing for me to do. I could not be
happy with one whom I did not esteem as well as love, and
by your conduct of late you have forfeited my good
opinion, and have destroyed my faith in you. I return
all your letters, and beg that you will send mine back to

me; I have also returned the presents you have made me at different times.

Believe me,
Yours very truly,
MARGARET WOODGATE.

From a Gentleman to a Lady to whom he is Engaged, asking her to put an end to the Engagement.

18, NORTH CRESCENT, S.W.,
January 10th, 18—,

MY DEAR EMILY,

I hesitate to write to you on a rather delicate subject, but I trust you will not be hurt or offended if I say that I fear our tastes are so opposite, that married life under such circumstances could not fail to result in unhappiness to both of us. Your heart is evidently set on the enjoyment of all the gaieties of life, while my ideas are centred in domestic quiet and repose. I have neither the means nor inclination to enter into the former, and you would hardly content yourself with the latter. You cannot but acknowledge the truth of this, and I have no doubt you will see the necessity of putting an end at once to an engagement that is in every way unsuitable.

Believe me, dear Miss Muir,
Very truly yours,
ALFRED COLE.

From a Gentleman to a Lady to whom he is Engaged, putting an end to the Engagement.

CHESTERFIELD TERRACE, HYDE PARK,
April 7th, 18—,

DEAR MISS BURTON,

I can but be aware that you desire to be released from your engagement, and since this is the case, pray consider that you are entirely free as far as any promise to me is concerned. I beg to return your letters, and with wishes for your future happiness,

Believe me, faithfully yours,
W. CARR.

From the Mother of a Young Lady to a Gentleman, breaking off his Engagement with her Daughter.

MARINE VILLA, WORTHING,
June 18th, 18—.

DEAR MR. MATTHEWS,

I am writing to you with my daughter's consent, and it is my painful duty to tell you that as there seems no prospect of your being able to make a home for her, I think it cruel and unfair to hold her to an engagement which has now lasted over two years. You have not fulfilled any of the promises you voluntarily made, and which induced me to sanction your attentions. I understand that your family are not inclined to do anything for you, and therefore I see nothing for my daughter but years of weary waiting, probably to end in ultimate disappointment.

If you have any regard for her welfare, you will, I am sure, release her from her present trying position, and accept my decision for her good without endeavouring to shake her resolution. I must ask you to send me a few lines of acquiescence; and with every wish for your success in life,

Believe me, dear Mr. Matthews,
Very truly yours,
AGNES CARTER.

From the Father of a Young Lady to a Gentleman, breaking off the Engagement.

PARK TERRACE, KENSINGTON,
October 4th, 18—.

DEAR SIR,

From circumstances that have come to my knowledge, I consider it my duty to break off the engagement between my daughter and yourself. I have desired her to hold no further communication with you, and I have been sufficiently explicit to convince her how unworthy you are of her affection and esteem. It is unnecessary for me to give you the reasons which have induced me to form this judgment, and I will only add that nothing you can say will alter my determination.

I am, Sir, yours faithfully,
E. R. FIELD.

To J. THOMAS, Esq.

From a Gentleman to a Lady to whom he is Engaged asking her Acceptance of a Present.

3, PARK TERRACE, KENSINGTON,
May 3rd, 18——.

MY DEAREST,

Will you accept the accompanying locket and wear it for my sake? I shall be much pleased to hear that you like it, and I only regret that I cannot present it in person, but I shall hope to see you ere long. Excuse a short letter to-day, and ever believe me,

Yours affectionately,
RICHARD BOYLE.

From a Young Lady to a Gentleman to whom she is Engaged, acknowledging a Present.

120, MARINA, ST. LEONARDS,
May 3rd, 18——.

DEAREST RICHARD,

Thank you so much for the beautiful locket I received this morning; I admire it immensely, and shall indeed be pleased to wear it for the sake of the dear giver. I should so like a good photo of you to put in it. Will you send me one when you next write, or better still, bring it yourself? You can imagine how greatly I am looking forward to your promised visit, and I only hope it will be soon; it seems so long since I have seen you. I trust, dearest Richard, you are quite well, and are not over-working yourself with too much writing as you told me you had been doing lately. How do you like your new quarters? Tell me everything about yourself. I think you know how interested I am in all that concerns you.

All are well at home; my aunt thinks of remaining here another three weeks.

I remain, dearest,
Yours lovingly,
CARRIE.

From the Mother of a Young Lady, announcing her Daughter's Engagement.

110, QUEEN'S TERRACE, KENSINGTON,
May 14th, 18—.

MY DEAR MRS. MORTLOCK,

I am sure you will be pleased to hear that darling Edith is engaged to be married to Mr. Lloyd ; he is the son of a very old friend of ours and is everything we could wish as a son-in-law, and it is delightful to see how happy the young people are in each other's society ; he is devoted to her and she is very fond of him. Had it not been so, in spite of our liking him so much, I doubt if we should have given our consent, as at present his prospects are not very good, and they will have to wait till next year before thinking of being married: thus you see it is not yet a matter for congratulations, but I did not wish you to hear the news from anyone but myself.

Believe me, dear Mrs. Mortlock, with kind regards from my husband and myself,

Very sincerely yours,

MABEL FINCH.

From the Mother of a Young Lady, announcing her Daughter's Engagement.

17, HEREFORD SQ. N.W.,
April 25th, 18—.

DEAR MRS. LONG,

I have an announcement to make which is a matter of great congratulation to my husband and myself: my daughter is about to make a very excellent marriage. She is engaged with our consent to Mr. Benson, who is in every way a most desirable *parti.* He has a large fortune, good connections, and is considered by all who know him to be a most honourable and high principled man. I think Ada is indeed a fortunate girl, and that her future is likely to realise all our fondest hopes. The engagement is not to be a long one, as Mr. Benson is anxious the marriage should take place at an early date, probably the first week in June.
Remember me kindly to Mr. Long.

Very sincerely yours,

HARRIET BURCH.

H

From a Young Lady to her Friend, announcing her Engagement.

WOODSTOCK HOUSE, MAIDA VALE.
May 3rd, 18——.

MY DEAR EVELYN,

I have some very good news to tell you about myself: I am engaged to be married to Mr. Charles Cross. I was not very much surprised at his proposing to me, as I fancied he liked me, from the constant attentions he has been paying me. You can imagine how happy I am; he is everything one would wish one's lover to be. I am sure you will think he is handsome. I do of course, and everyone says he is very clever. He is five years older than I am, which mamma thinks is an advantage. I hope you will be one of my bridesmaids, dear Evelyn; we are to be married very soon. He has taken a nice house, and you must be one of our first visitors. Papa and mamma are delighted at my prospects, and think Charlie will make me the best of husbands.

With best love, believe me,

Your ever affectionate,

LAURA FIELD.

From a Gentleman to a Friend, announcing his Engagement.

8, ADDISON VALE, KENSINGTON,
June 30th, 18—.

MY DEAR HAMMOND,

Perhaps you will be surprised to hear that I am going to be married, and that I shall want your services on the occasion as best man, but I will give you due notice when the day is fixed. In the meantime you may if you please congratulate me, as I consider myself to be a very lucky fellow. She is one of the nicest girls in the world—Fanny Arkwright. I get on very well with her people, and my future father-in-law is inclined to be very liberal about money matters.

Yours ever,

H. SALTER.

From a Lady to the Mother of a Bride elect, offering her Congratulations.

7, MONMOUTH TERRACE, W.,
June 1st, 18—.

MY DEAR MRS. OSBORNE,
We were charmed to hear of your daughter's engagement, and sincerely wish her every happiness; please tell her so with my love. It must be a great source of pleasure to you to know that she is going to make so satisfactory a marriage, one of which you and her father so highly approve. I shall hope to make the acquaintance of your future son-in-law at an early opportunity, and you must tell me when the wedding is to take place, as should I not be in town at that time, I might yet embody my good wishes in the form of a wedding present.
With kind remembrances to you all,
Sincerely yours,
MARY BISHOP.

From a Lady to the Mother of a Bride elect, offering Congratulations on a Reported Engagement.

IVY VILLA, PUTNEY,
March 12th, 18—.

MY DEAR MRS. WHEELER,
I hope I am not premature in offering my congratulations on your daughter's engagement, having heard the news from two reliable sources. I cannot resist telling you how interested I am in this event, and that she has my best wishes for her future happiness. I can fancy how sorry you will be to lose her, but no doubt the thought that she will be comfortably settled in life will in a measure reconcile you to parting with her; still of course you will miss her very much at first.
Pray say everything that is most kind to her from me and believe me,
Very truly yours,
E. GIBSON.

From a Lady to the Mother of a Bridegroom, offering Congratulations on his Engagement.

WESTON VICARAGE, WINCHESTER,
June 12th, 18—.

MY DEAR MRS. ELLIS,

I understand your son is engaged to be married, and I must offer you and him my kindest congratulations. I hope the marriage is one you thoroughly approve of, and that the young lady is all you could wish and that she will make him very happy. Much as you may rejoice with him, it will no doubt be a trial to you to feel that another has more than taken your place; but you love him so dearly and are so unselfish that you will I am sure think rather of his happiness than of your own feelings. I have not heard if the bride elect has any fortune; I hope she has for your son's sake, as in these matter-of-fact days young people require so much to begin housekeeping upon, far more so than in my young days.

Please give my kind regards to your son, and with love to yourself,

Believe me,
Your affectionate friend,
ALICE RIVERS.

From a Young Lady, Congratulating a Friend on her Engagement.

HEATH COTTAGE, WANDSWORTH,
June 9th, 18—.

MY DEAR DORA,

I must tell you how pleased I was to hear of your engagement, and hasten to offer you my warmest congratulations. Do tell me all about your *fiancé*, and whether it is to be a long engagement. I need not ask if you are very happy, as I am sure you would not have accepted anyone to whom you were not sincerely attached. You will doubtless have a great many letters to answer from friends and relatives just now, all desirous of wishing you joy, but still I hope you will find time to write me a few lines soon.

With kindest love,
Yours most affectionately,
BLANCHE WEBB.

From a Married Lady, Congratulating a Young Lady on her Engagement.

LYME LODGE, STREATHAM,
August 2nd, 18—.

MY DEAR EMILY,

It was with much pleasure I heard of your engagement to Mr. Williams, as from all I can learn he seems in
every way worthy of you; and I hope, my dear child, you
thoroughly understand the responsibilities of the position
you will be called upon to take as his wife. I doubt not
you will study his happiness in all things, and that you
will find in him a kind and devoted husband.

I can fancy how pleased your dear father must be at
your happy prospects, which appear to be without a drawback, as I understand Mr. Williams is very well off. Perhaps I may see you next week; in the meantime accept my
kind love and good wishes, and believe me to remain,

Your very affectionate friend,

ANNA JOHNSTONE.

From the Mother of a Gentleman to a Young Lady by whom her Son has just been Accepted.

PLAS ENNID, WREXHAM,
December 2nd, 18—.

MY DEAR AGNES,

My son has asked me to write to you, and although
I have not had the pleasure of seeing you, yet from all he
says of you I feel sure that he has chosen wisely. He has
always been the best of sons to me—so affectionate, tender-
hearted, and considerate ; and you will understand something of the pride I feel in him, and how dearly I love him,
and how anxious I am that the one who is to be his wife
should value him at his true worth. It would be a great
pleasure to me if your parents would allow you to pay me
a little visit, as I much wish to make the acquaintance of
my future daughter-in-law.

My son has shown me your photograph, so I have some
idea as to what you are like. He tells me how charming
you are, and that he is certain I shall not be disappointed

in you when we meet. Dear Agnes, my boy's happiness is in your keeping, and I trust and pray you may be to him all his fond mother could wish.

With kind love I remain,
Your affectionate
SUSAN SMYTHE.

From a Young Lady to the Mother of the Gentleman to whom she is Engaged.

5, CHESTER TERRACE, S.W.,
December 4th, 18—.

MY DEAR MRS. SMYTHE,

I thought it so kind of you to write to me. I cannot help feeling a little shy in answering your letter, but I trust we shall not long remain strangers to each other. Claude has often talked of you to me, and is so anxious that we should meet; but I am sorry to say Mamma cannot spare me just now, otherwise I should have been very pleased to have accepted your kind invitation. I quite appreciate all that you say in praise of your son, and I think I love him almost as much as even you could wish, and indeed you may trust me to do all in my power to make him happy. Thanking you again for your kind letter, believe me,

Affectionately yours,
AGNES TRAVERS.

From a Married Sister of a Gentleman to the Lady to whom he is Engaged.

3, CLARENDON TERRACE, BAYSWATER,
July 14th, 18—.

MY DEAR MISS BARLOW,

My brother has told me of his engagement to you, and I write to say how much I rejoice in his happiness. I have seen very little of him lately, as he has been a good deal away, but I know what a dear good fellow he is, and I am sure he will make the woman who loves him the kindest of husbands. I shall hope to make your acquaintance very soon, and I trust we shall become great friends.

With kindest regards,
Very sincerely yours,
GEORGINA PRATT.

From a Young Lady to the Married Sister of the Gentleman to whom she is Engaged.

EASTMOUNT, TORQUAY,
July 17th, 18—.

DEAR MRS. PRATT,

Very many thanks for your kind note. I shall look forward with much pleasure to being introduced to you and to all the members of dear Robert's family. I do so hope you will like me; I am most anxious you should, for his sake as well as for my own. Mamma and I expect to be in town the end of this month. We are to stay at my uncle's house, 18, Edinburgh Place, S.W., and I shall ask your brother to bring me to see you as soon as we arrive.

Believe me, dear Mrs. Pratt,

Very sincerely yours,

JESSIE BARLOW.

From a Bride elect asking a Young Lady to be her Bridesmaid.

5, MANCHESTER GARDENS, S.W.,
June 13th, 18—.

MY DEAR MISS BOYCE,

My marriage is to take place on the 15th of next month, and I write to say it would give me much pleasure if you would be one of my bridesmaids. I thought of having eight—my two sisters of course, Mr. Eton's sister and a cousin of his, the two Miss Websters, yourself if you will consent, and Miss Norton.

We have not yet decided about the dresses, but I will let you know what we settle upon as soon as I have your answer. We expect Miss Eton here to-morrow to talk the matter over with us.

With love to yourself and kind regards to Mrs. Boyce, believe me,

Very sincerely yours,

GRACE CALLENDER.

CHAPTER IX.

FAMILY LETTERS.

Complimentary Letter to an Aunt.

5, EAST STREET, CROYDON,
July 8th, 18—.

MY DEAR AUNT,

I hope you and uncle John have not thought me neglectful in not writing to you before this, but beyond asking after you both and hoping you are quite well, I felt I had nothing to write about. I lead as you know such a quiet life and the days so resemble each other that I can hardly distinguish them apart. I ought perhaps to be glad of this, as family news when it has to be told is seldom a matter of rejoicing; quite the contrary, it generally forebodes trouble and sorrow—at least I have found it so.

The east winds have been very trying to my mother lately, but I am happy to say she is fairly well and able to go out every day. She sends her love to you and hopes to have the pleasure of seeing you and my dear uncle before long.

How is your work society getting on? I suppose your school treat will take place next month. I can imagine how busy uncle John must be just now in his garden. Are the bees thriving? and how do the new glass hives answer? Has he been making any fresh experiments?

Please give him my best love, and with much to yourself,

Believe me, dear aunt,
Your affectionate niece,
FLORENCE STEDMAN.

Complimentary Letter to an Uncle.

10, NORTH STREET, NORWICH,
Dec. 8th, 18—.

MY DEAR UNCLE JOHN,

We have been expecting a letter from you for some time past, and cannot help fearing that you are perhaps suffering from your old enemy the gout. I trust however that I am mistaken, and that you will be able to give a very good account of your health when you do write, which I hope will be soon. I send you this week's Athenæum, and have marked a paragraph in it which I thought would interest you, relating to Wedgwood ware.

I am making you another pair of slippers, which I hope you will like; they will be quite ready by Christmas. How pleased we should all be if you would spend your Christmas with us this year.

With best love from us all, believe me, dear uncle John,

Your very affectionate niece,

GEORGINA WELLS.

Complimentary Letter to a Mother-in-Law.

ST. MARY'S STREET, STAFFORD,
October 10th, 18—.

MY DEAR MRS. CLARKE,

George and I are anxious to know if you have returned home yet, and how you have enjoyed your stay at the sea-side. We received your last letter dated Sept 3rd, and have been a little surprised at not hearing from you since.

I hardly know where to write to you, but suppose this letter will be forwarded from Eastbourne. George is pretty well and is looking forward to his holiday, which has been postponed this year on account, I believe, of extra work in the office, but we do not regret this as we have had such very stormy weather the last three weeks.

The children unite with me in love to dear grand-mamma.

Believe me,

Yours affectionately,

MARGARET CLARKE.

Complimentary Letter to a Father-in-Law.

ST. JOHN'S TERRACE, W.,
Feb. 10th, 18—.

DEAR MR. NORTON,

We were so glad to learn from your last letter that you have been quite well in spite of the severe weather we have lately experienced, and that you are in such good spirits. How wise you are not to let the small worries of life depress you. I wish I had a little of your philosophy; as it is, I fear I take things too much to heart, and am inclined to allow trifles to vex me. You set us all such a good example by your unvaried cheerfulness.

I suppose you were very much interested in Tuesday's debate, as you are such a keen politician; but I will not express my opinion on it, gathered second-hand from my husband, in case it should run counter to yours. This you may call cowardice on my part, but it is really discretion.

With kindest love from Fred and myself, believe me, dear Mr. Norton,

Yours affectionately,
H. G. NORTON.

Complimentary Letter to a Son-in-Law.

5, GROVE ROAD, N.W.,
Nov. 10th, 18—.

MY DEAR GEORGE,

I was very glad to hear such a good account of you all from Carrie, as, although it is some time since I have been to your house, still I must always feel deeply interested in all that concerns you and yours.

Perhaps I was foolish in fancying that the advice I offered was unpalatable to you: it is, I know, the received idea that a mother-in-law's interference is never welcome, however reasonable may be her remarks; but believe me, dear George, what I said I meant in good part, and had no intention of censuring or criticising any arrangement of yours. I should have expressed the same opinion to any friend of mine under similar circumstances had I been consulted. The fact of your being my son-in-law induced me to imagine that I might speak frankly to you without fear of giving offence; indeed, I regard you as a son, and you must not be too prone to resent words my motherly affection prompts me to say.

With kindest love to Carrie and yourself, and many kisses to my dear little grandchildren,

Believe me,
Yours affectionately,
E. BARLOW.

Complimentary Letter to a Daughter-in-Law.

5, KENT PLACE, N.E.
July 5th, 18—.

MY DEAR SOPHIE,

I must tell you how much I enjoyed my little visit to you last week, the first I have paid to you in your new home, and I trust many years of happiness are in store for you and my dear son. He tells me that he has in you the most considerate and affectionate of wives : I sincerely rejoice that it is so. I have seen many an unhappy marriage owing to thoughtlessness and extravagance on the part of the wife, that I am indeed glad to think my boy is so fortunate in his choice. His limited means call for the most careful domestic management, and not a little self-denial, and it is so easy when first commencing house-keeping to run into more expense than one's income justi-fies ; but this error I am sure you will carefully guard against, and will remember what strict supervision is required in the smallest domestic details.

I have learnt this from experience, dear Sophie, which I have found to be the best of teachers.

With kindest love to yourself and my son,
Believe me, yours affectionately,
M. DALE.

Complimentary Letter to a Sister-in-Law.

ROSE COTTAGE, TULSE HILL,
Aug. 4th, 18—.

MY DEAR ELLA,

I am not quite sure whether I owe you a letter or whether I wrote last; however there need be no ceremony between us in this matter, and I will take for granted that my letter will be welcome whichever way it is. I hope you and Ernest are all the better for your week at Brighton. A breath of sea air generally does one good; even if one is in the best of health, the change is beneficial to the spirits, which require refreshing and bracing as much as does the poor body when out of condition, and you have had no little anxiety lately in many ways.

Do not take the trouble to write yourself if you are particularly occupied just now, but let me have a little message from you through Hilda, whom I often hear from; indeed, she is quite the best correspondent I have and gives me all the family news.

With kindest love to yourself and Ernest,
Believe me, dear Ella,
Yours very affectionately,
EDITH ALLEN.

Complimentary Letter to a Brother-in-Law.

17, COURT ROAD, S.W.,
July 20th, 18—.

MY DEAR PHILIP,

My husband is a very bad correspondent and has, I have discovered, allowed your last kind letter to remain unanswered; so I will try and take his place as far as I can and ask you to accept me as his substitute. Your news was most interesting to us both. You seem to have had a very pleasant holiday; we quite envied you, and I very much wish Edward could have gone with you, if only for three weeks, but he is so hard worked that there seems no chance of his having even a day's holiday until the end of the season. He is however, I am happy to say, quite well. I suppose you will be back about the end of next month; if my advice is worth anything, I should say do not make the return journey too quickly, but take a fair amount of rest by the way: it is a great mistake to travel night and day after weeks of complete repose and quiet, and is calculated to neutralise all the benefit derived from change of climate and scene.

With kindest love from us both,
Believe me, dear Philip,
Yours affectionately,
ANNIE CHURCH.

From a Youth to his Father, respecting Dislike of his Present Occupation.

88, LINCOLN'S INN FIELDS,
April 10th, 18—.

MY DEAR FATHER,

I am afraid you will be disappointed at what I am about to say, but I hope after due consideration you will not think I am altogether wrong in frankly stating my great dislike to office work. I have now been here nearly six months, and I find this employment as little to my taste as on first commencing it. I have tried my best to become used to it, but I am quite sure I shall never get on in this line of life.

I should be very glad to talk the matter over with you; it is not that I am afraid of work, only my present occupation does not and never will suit me.

I have given it a fair trial, and have put off writing to you on the subject as long as possible; but as there is no chance of my changing my mind, I thought further delay would be useless. I shall hope to hear from you in a day or two, dear father, and with love to all at home,

Believe me,
Your affectionate son,
H. MILLAR.

To a Married Sister, soliciting her Husband's Influence.

8, MADINA VILLAS, CLAPHAM,
June 10th, 18—.

MY DEAR CHARLOTTE,

I have not written to you lately as I have been rather out of spirits, besides being very much occupied.

I am beginning to discover there is little chance of promotion for me in this house, and that it is almost time I should look about me for something better. Do you think your husband would interest himself for me in any way, and would you dislike speaking to him on the subject? I do not exactly know the extent of his influence, or indeed if he possesses any, but I thought from the responsible position he holds with Messrs. Kent, he might perhaps know of some opening that would suit me. I have never as yet spoken to him about my own affairs, and if on your part you feel any reluctance in making this request, pray do not hesitate to tell me so.

Charlie seems very happy at school, but is looking forward to spending his holidays with you.

I suppose Ethel's marriage will take place in the autumn from what she says.

With kind love, believe me,

Your affectionate brother,

HERBERT READ.

From a Sister to an Elder Brother, respecting an Advance of Money.

75, LADBROOKE ROAD,
July 2nd, 18—.

MY DEAR WILLIAM,

I have a great favour to ask, which I trust you will grant if you can do so without any inconvenience to yourself.

I have just received a very pressing invitation to go with Mrs. Meadows and her daughter to Geneva, and to make a tour with them in Switzerland, which would be quite a new experience to me, as I have never yet been abroad. I could not of course promise to join them until I had consulted you about it, dear Willie, and asked you whether you would make me a small advance to meet the necessary expenses of the journey, and to purchase the few things I should require before starting.

Would you think £20 too much to spare at the present time? I have a little money left, but not enough to justify my accepting this invitation without some little help from you. You have always been so kind and considerate towards me, that I know you will gladly give me this pleasure if it lies in your power to do so. It seems a long time since I have seen you, or even heard from you, but I know you are so much engaged, that a letter from you is hardly to be expected, unless there is something especially interesting to be communicated.

With kindest love, believe me, dear Willie,

Your affectionate sister,

LUCY E. MARTIN.

To a Cousin, expressing Christmas Good Wishes.

8, FERN VILLAS, GUNNERSBURY.
Dec. 23rd, 18—.

MY DEAR EDITH,

I wish you and dear aunt Lucy a merry Christmas, and many happy New Years.

It is a long time since we have met; circumstances do not bring us together—quite the contrary; and were it not for the annually returning season of Christmastide, I fear we should almost drop out of each other's recollection. I am therefore glad of the opportunity of inquiring after you and dear aunt Lucy, and trust that you are both pretty well. I fear she is rather dreading the severe weather which is prophesied to be in store for us, but prophecies are not always fulfilled, and in any case, I hope she will not have a return of her old complaint, bronchitis.

With kindest love and wishes to you both,

Your affectionate cousin,

MABEL CLARKE.

From a Young Man to his Guardian, asking for an increased Allowance.

5, GEORGE ST., S.W.,
March 17th, 18—.

DEAR MR. ATKINSON,

I am very reluctant to ask you to make me a further allowance, but the fact is, I find it impossible to meet the necessary expenses that I am compelled to incur, on the sum at present allowed to me, and, as I know how much you disapprove of my getting into debt, I thought it best to write to you frankly on the subject, and ask you to see what you could do for me. I should be perfectly satisfied with an additional £50 per annum, and I trust you will not think this request unreasonable.

I beg to remain,

Very truly yours,

R. REYNOLDS.

From a Guardian, reproaching his Ward with Extravagance.

7, CHURCH HOUSE, WAKEFIELD,
March 19*th,* 18—.

MY DEAR RICHARD,

It is very painful to me to refuse a request of yours, but were I to comply with it, I should only be encouraging you in extravagance. Your poor father considered the sum at present allowed you amply sufficient for your wants, and I do not feel justified in acting contrary to his expressed wishes. However, I have no objection to making you a present of £20 to meet any pressing claim, but I must again warn you that it is imperative you should restrict your expenses within the limits of your allowance, and this can readily be done by giving a little more attention to details, and by being less thoughtless in your every day expenditure.

I am, dear Richard,
Your sincere friend,
E. ATKINSON.

From a Young Man, excusing his Extravagance.

17, EGLINTON ROAD, N.W.,
Dec. 20*th,* 18—.

MY DEAR UNCLE,

Thank you for your very kind letter. I am deeply sorry to have occasioned you so much anxiety, and am most grateful to you for your timely aid. Believe me in future I will endeavour to give you no further cause for complaint, and I can only regret that I should have allowed myself to be led into such thoughtless extravagance. You may depend upon my following your advice, and proving myself worthy of your generous kindness.

I am, dear uncle,
Your affectionate nephew,
H. BAXTER.

CHAPTER X.

CHILDREN'S LETTERS.

From a Young Lady at School to her Mother.

WEST GROVE ACADEMY, BRIGHTON,
April 3rd, 18—.

MY DEAREST MOTHER,

I have now been here nearly a week, and like my school life better than I did at first. I share a bedroom with three young ladies. Miss Barker, the eldest of the three, is very kind to me, and we are great friends already; she is only a year older than I am. To-day is half-holiday, but it has been raining all the morning, which prevents our going out; however, I have a great many interesting books lent me, and the girls appear to be very good-natured. In my next letter I will tell you how I get on in my classes. I am afraid I am very backward in French, as I am placed with the youngest girls in the school. I hope you will not forget to send me a basket next week according to promise. Please give my best love to dear papa and Johnnie and Minnie, and with the same to yourself, dearest mother,

Believe me,

Your very affectionate daughter,

MARION.

From a Little Boy at School to his Sister.

MOUNT ARARAT HOUSE, CHICHESTER,
August 7th, 18—.

DEAR JANE,

We break up on Thursday week. I hope my rabbits are well, and my pony also. How is your garden looking? I will help you a bit in it when I come home. We are going to have a game at cricket, so goodbye. Give my love to all. I hope mamma got my letter.

Your affectionate brother,

CHARLIE.

From a Little Girl to her Brother at School.

17, CHICHESTER SQ., S.W.,
October 4th, 18—.

DEAR JOHNNIE,

I miss you very much. I have no one to play with me now. How do you like being at school? are the lessons very difficult? are there any nice boys you like? Do tell me all about it; what you have for dinner, what hour you go to bed, and what games you play at, and how long you are allowed to play.

Papa and mamma send their best love.

I am,
Your affectionate sister,
CARRIE.

From a Little Girl at School to her Mother respecting her Studies.

WESTWOOD HOUSE, BATH,
Oct. 10th, 18—.

MY DEAR MAMMA,

I am very sorry indeed Miss Strong has had to complain of me, but I do try to learn my very difficult lessons, and when I cannot do so I cry until my head aches. Dear mamma, I wish I need not learn German until next term, and then perhaps I should get on better with my French lessons.

Please give my love to dear papa, and tell him I would not make him unhappy if I could help it, but I have so much to learn every day, and all the girls in my class are older than I am, and have been much longer at school.

I am, dear mamma,
Your very affectionate daughter,
NELLIE.

From a Little Boy to his Papa.

5, CLARENDON SQ., W.,
April 6th, 18—.

MY DEAR PAPA,

I hope to see you soon, you have been away a very long time; when are you coming back again? I have to be a good boy, and Miss Osborne says I have been most attentive at my lessons. Dear mamma will send this little letter with hers.

I am, dear papa,
Your affectionate son,
FREDERICK PEACH.

From a Little Boy to his Grandpapa.

7, BEECH TERRACE, SOUTHSEA,
August 4th, 18—.

DEAR GRANDPAPA,

I hope you are quite well. I wish you many happy returns of your birthday, and I send you a little paper knife which I bought with my own money, and I hope you will like it and use it; it cuts beautifully. Annie is going to send you a present also, but I must not tell you what it is to be; she made it herself.

I am, dear grandpapa,
Your affectionate grandson,
ERNEST HARVEY.

From a Little Boy to his Uncle.

8, LUDLOW TERRACE,
May 3rd, 18—.

MY DEAR UNCLE FRED,

Thank you very much indeed for the beautiful watch you sent me on my birthday. Mamma says I may wear it, but I must not wind it up until I am older, and she keeps the key for me. I have learnt to tell the time by it; it is now a quarter past three and we are going out for a walk in the park, so good-bye, dear uncle Fred.

We all send you our best love. I am,
Your affectionate nephew,
CHARLES RAYMOND.

From a Little Girl to her Mamma.

17, COVENTRY SQ., S.W.,
Nov. 8th, 18—.

MY DEAR MAMMA,

Aunt Ellen is writing to you, but I thought you would also like a little letter from me. I am enjoying myself very much, everyone is so kind to me, but I must

I A

tell you all I have seen when I come home. I am longing
to see you, dear mamma, and with best love and kisses to
you and dear papa, I remain,
Your affectionate daughter,
SOPHIE.

From a Little Girl to her Grandmamma.
7, NEWPORT STREET, BRIGHTON,
Nov. 18*th,* 18—.

MY DEAR GRANDMAMMA,
How very kind of you to send me such a beautiful
doll. Mamma has given me a cradle to put it in at night,
and I mean to take it out walking with me every day.
Dear mamma says the next time she comes to see you she
will bring me with her; I hope it will be soon.
With best love, dear grandmamma,
I remain,
Your affectionate granddaughter,
BESSIE.

To a Little Girl, asking her to Tea.
ELM HOUSE, READING,
Dec. 4*th,* 18—.

DEAR MINNIE,
Next Wednesday is my birthday. Mamma says I
may have a little tea party, and I am to write the notes of
invitation myself. I hope your mamma will let you come.
We shall have tea at half past four, and games and dancing
after tea.
I am, your affectionate friend,
EDITH WOODHOUSE.

From a Little Girl accepting Invitation to Tea.
5, STANHOPE TERRACE, READING,
Dec. 5*th,* 18—.

MY DEAR EDITH,
Mamma says I may come to tea with you next Wednesday, and I shall be very happy to see you. I wonder if
you will have many birthday presents. Mamma is going to
send you one which I think you will like.
I am, dear Edith,
Your affectionate,
MINNIE MOORE.

From a Little Girl to her Mother.

BRAMBLE HOUSE, WARWICK,
June 7th, 18—.

DARLING MOTHER,

Papa and I miss you very much indeed, and I hope to hear in your next letter that aunt Harriet is better, and that you will be able to come home in a day or two. Papa is writing to you by this post. I am going out for a ride with him presently. Nurse says the children are very good and happy. Flo cried a little last night because she could not say goodnight to you, but she soon went off to sleep while nurse told her a pretty story about a good little girl who did everything her papa and mamma wished. Goodbye, dear darling mother.

Your loving daughter,
KATE.

CHAPTER XI.

SERVANTS' LETTERS.

From a Butler to his Master, giving Notice

THE GRANGE, DORKING,
July 4th, 18—.

HONOURED SIR,
I take the liberty of saying that I wish to leave your service this day month. I have the offer of a situation as butler to the Earl of Carlton, providing that I can have a good character from my present employer.

I trust that I have given you satisfaction during the two years that I have lived with you, and that you will be kind enough to recommend me.

I am, Sir,
Your humble servant,
JOHN SILVER.

From a Cook to her Mistress, giving Notice.

BURY HOUSE, TAUNTON,
Dec. 18th, 18—.

HONOURED MADAM,
I take the liberty of writing to you to inform you that I wish to give notice to leave your service this day month, but should you not be suited by that time, I should be happy to stay a week or two longer, to avoid putting you to any inconvenience.

My reason for leaving is that I wish for a change, as I find the country very dull. The family being so much away, I have little opportunity of keeping up and improving my cooking, but in all other respects I am thoroughly satisfied with my situation.

I remain, Madam,
Your humble servant,

From a Cook to a Lady, asking her to Recommend her.

LONDON ROAD COTTAGES, HAMMERSMITH,
Dec. 3rd, 18—.

HONOURED MADAM,

I hope you will excuse my troubling you, but may I ask if you would have any objection to saying what you could in my favour to Mrs. Leigh, who will engage me as cook, if I can obtain a satisfactory reference as to my respectability and character. I thought as I had formerly lived in your service and as my family was well known to you, you would perhaps allow me to refer to you. I am aware that I cannot ask you for a character, having received one from you on leaving your service; but unfortunately on leaving my last situation the housekeeper refused to give me one on account of my having lost my temper with her, she having been previously very violent in her language towards me.

I mentioned this circumstance to Mrs. Leigh, who says she will overlook it if the answer from my former mistress to her inquiries was satisfactory.

I shall be very grateful to you, honoured Madam, if you will grant this request.

I beg to remain,
Your humble servant,
CAROLINE BARRETT.

From a Housemaid to a Lady, Applying for a Situation.

THE FARM COTTAGE, BURWELL,
Sept. 8th, 18—.

HONOURED MADAM,

I understand from Mrs. Elsden that you are in want of a housemaid, and I venture to apply for the situation. I have been living for the last two years with Mrs. Ford, The Terrace, Richmond, who will give me an excellent character. I am 23 years of age and am strong and active. I received £14 a year wages and all found. I should be very happy to come over and see you, any day you may please to name.

I am, your humble servant,
ALICE RICE.

From a Housemaid Accepting a Situation.

5, GREEN ST., IPSWICH,
May 16th, 18—.

HONOURED MADAM,

I received your letter this morning, and beg to say I shall be very pleased to accept your situation.

I shall be quite ready to come to you on Tuesday, the 21st, and will start by the 7.30 train, from Ipswich.

Your humble servant,
ELIZA HODGERS.

From a Parlour-maid to a Lady, excusing herself from taking a Situation.

HIGH STREET, BURY ST. EDMUNDS,
March 4th, 18—.

HONOURED MADAM,

I hope you will pardon my saying that I wish to decline your situation, as I fear that the work would be too heavy for me. I had not sufficiently considered this before engaging to take the place of parlour-maid in your family, but I feel that I am not strong enough for all that would be required of me in that capacity.

I beg to remain,
Your humble servant,
HARRIET JAGGARD.

From a Working Housekeeper to her Master.

78, BRUNSWICK SQ., BRIGHTON,
Oct. 4th, 18—.

HONOURED SIR,

Messrs. Wright & Robins gave me up the key of this house on my arrival yesterday afternoon, and this morning one of their clerks went over it with me as you desired. He has made out a list of things which require to be put in order before the house can be re-let. I think it has been left in a very dirty condition; the carpets in the dining-room and study are much worn, many of the drawing-room chairs have been removed into the bed-rooms and the coverings torn. The springs of the large sofa in the drawing-room are broken, and altogether the furniture has been treated very badly. I do not know how to make the kitchens look clean, and the small scullery has been used as a coal cellar.

I wish, Sir, you could see all the mischief that has been done; however, I will do my best to get the house in order by the end of next week.

Your humble servant,
MARTHA CHALLIS.

From a Nurse to her Mistress.

17, WARRIOR SQ., ST. LEONARDS,
August 8th, 18—.

HONOURED MADAM,

I write to inform you that the dear children are quite well. Miss Nina has almost lost her cough, and Master Robert has a wonderful appetite compared to what he had when he left home. They all send their best love to dear Papa and Mamma. We are out over four hours a day. Miss Ethel has a sea-water bath every morning. The landlady cooks the meals very well and comes to me for orders every day. I am very particular in attending to all your directions.

I enclose the list of things wanted for the young ladies which you desired me to send. I beg to remain,

Your humble servant,
EMMA SMITH.

An Offer of Marriage from a Butler to a Cook.

105, MANCHESTER SQ., W.,
April 15th, 18—.

DEAR MISS CLARKE,

I have been anxious for some time past to make my feelings known to you, but have not had an opportunity of doing so. I therefore think it best not to delay any longer but to tell you by letter that I very much wish to make you my wife, if you think you could be happy with me. We have seen each other so often the last two years, I am quite sure I should never like anyone but you; and I want you to say you have a favourable opinion of me, and that your heart is mine, my dear Ellen. If this is so, the sooner we are married the better.

The legacy of £100 I received from my late master, added to my own savings of the last ten years, will enable me to take a lodging-house in a good situation, and I have already seen one which I think would answer very well, but I cannot decide upon anything until I know whether you will accept me as your husband, and if I have not greatly mistaken your sentiments I believe you will.

I remain, my dear Ellen,
Your fond lover,
T. BAKER.

From a Cook, accepting an Offer of Marriage.

125, CADOGAN GARDENS, W.,
April 17th, 18—.

DEAR MR. BAKER,
I hasten to answer your kind letter. You have not mistaken my feelings : I have a great respect and esteem for you joined to a sincere affection, and from what I know of you, I feel sure you would make me a good and kind husband, and therefore I have no hesitation in accepting your offer. I am very much flattered by your good opinion of me, and as your wife, I will do everything in my power to continue to deserve it.

I hardly know what to say about being married at once, as I am very comfortable in my present situation, and am putting by a little money every year; but as you are thinking of taking a lodging-house at once, I had better hear what you have to say before making up my mind either way.

Hoping to see you very soon,
I am, dear Tom,
With kind love,
Your truly affectionate,
ELLEN CLARKE.

From a Lady's Maid to her Lover, breaking off her Engagement.

60, PORCHESTER SQUARE, W.,
June 26th, 18—.

DEAR WILLIAM,
I have been endeavouring to make up my mind for some time past to write to you on a very painful subject. I am much grieved to tell you that I think our engagement must be broken off.

You must be aware of the reason of this decision, and I

need not say more except to entreat you for your own sake to give up your unsteady ways. I shall always be glad to hear of your welfare, but no persuasion would induce me to marry a man who had taken to such evil courses as you have done the last four months, as there could be no possible happiness for a woman whose husband spent all his earnings in drink.

I am, dear William,

Your wellwisher,

ANNE LEE.

CHAPTER XII.

NOTES AND LETTERS OF INVITATIONS, ANSWERS, AND POSTPONEMENTS.

From a Lady, Inviting a Married Couple to Dinner.

7, CHICHESTER GARDENS, N.W.,
May 10th, 18—.

DEAR MRS. HAMILTON,

Will you and Mr. Hamilton give us the pleasure of your company at dinner on Thursday the 24th instant at ¼ to 8 o'clock?

Very sincerely yours,
E. MORTON.

_____

From a Lady, accepting an Invitation for herself and husband to Dinner.

5, ENFIELD TERRACE, N.W.,
May 13th, 18—.

DEAR MRS. MORTON,

It will give us much pleasure to accept your kind invitation to dine with you on Thursday the 24th instant.

Very truly yours,
G. HAMILTON.

_____

From a Lady, declining an Invitation for herself and husband to Dinner.

5, ENFIELD TERRACE. N.W.,
May 13th, 18—.

DEAR MRS. MORTON,

I very much regret that a prior engagement will prevent our having the pleasure of dining with you on Thursday the 24th instant.

Very truly yours,
E. HAMILTON.

From a Lady, inviting a Married Couple to Dinner.

PARK HOUSE, BATH,
Dec. 6th, 18—.

DEAR MRS. WHITE,

We should be very pleased if you and Mr. White would dine with us on Wednesday the 14th instant at 7 o'clock. It will be quite a small party, as we have only asked Mr. and Mrs. Churchill and Mr. and Miss Blake. We trust you will be disengaged and able to give us the pleasure of your company.

Very truly yours,
H. NORTON.

From a Lady, accepting Invitation for herself and husband to Dinner.

18, MARINE CRESCENT, BATH,
Dec. 7th, 18—.

DEAR MRS. NORTON,

We have much pleasure in accepting your kind invitation to dine with you on the 14th instant. I was so sorry to miss seeing you on Tuesday; we had gone for a long drive to Whittleby and did not return till after five. I hope to be more fortunate the next time you call.

Believe me,
Very truly yours,
C. WHITE.

From a Lady, declining Invitation for herself and husband to Dinner.

18, MARINE CRESCENT, BATH,
Dec. 7th, 18—.

DEAR MRS. NORTON,

We are extremely sorry that we are unable to accept your kind invitation to dinner, but we are going up to town on the 10th of this month, and shall not return home until after the 18th, when I shall hope to come and see you.

Very truly yours,
C. WHITE.

To a Lady, Inviting her to Dinner.

7, STAFFORD GARDENS, S.W.,
June 6th, 18—.

DEAR MISS YOUNG,

Will you excuse a short notice, and give us the pleasure of your company at dinner on Wednesday, the 9th instant, at 8 o'clock? It will be quite a small party, as I have only asked a few people.

Believe me,
Very sincerely yours,
H. CLEMENTS.

From a Lady, accepting an Invitation to Dinner.

17, BEAUFORT STREET, S.W.,
June 7th, 18—.

DEAR MRS. CLEMENTS,

I have much pleasure in accepting your kind invitation to dinner for Wednesday the 9th instant. Are you going to Mrs. Chester's to-morrow afternoon? if so, I shall hope to meet you there.

Believe me,
Very sincerely yours,
KATE YOUNG.

From a Lady, declining an Invitation to Dinner.

17, BEAUFORT STREET, S.W.,
June 7th, 18—.

DEAR MRS. CLEMENTS,

I am sorry I cannot have the pleasure of dining with you on Wednesday next, but I am going with my sister-in-law to a Garden party on that day and fear we shall not be back before nine. It is very kind of you to think of me, and I much regret that I am thus prevented from accepting your invitation.

Very sincerely yours,
KATE YOUNG.

To a Gentleman, Inviting him to Dinner.

7, STAFFORD GARDENS, S.W.,
Tuesday, June 24th, 18—.

DEAR MR. BROOK,
We should be very pleased if you would dine with us on Saturday next, the 28th instant, at 8 o'clock, if disengaged.

Very truly yours,
H. CLEMENTS.

To a Gentleman, Inviting him to Dinner.

7, STAFFORD GARDENS, S.W.,
Tuesday, June 24th, 18—.

DEAR MR. LOVEL,
Will you give us the pleasure of your company at dinner on Friday, the 27th instant, at ¼ to 8 o'clock? Please excuse this short notice, as we have only just heard you were in town.

Very truly yours,
H. CLEMENTS.

From a Gentleman, accepting Invitation to Dinner.

192, EBURY ST., W.,
June 25th, 18—.

DEAR MRS. CLEMENTS,
I shall be very happy to dine with you on Friday next, the 27th. I should have had the pleasure of calling on you ere this, but I have been so much occupied since my return to town, that I have not had a moment to pay any such civility to my friends.

Very truly yours,
E. LOVEL.

From a Gentleman, declining an Invitation to Dinner.

192, EBURY ST., W.,
June 25th, 18—.

DEAR MRS. CLEMENTS,
It would have given me great pleasure to have accepted your kind invitation to dine with you on Friday,

the 27th, but unfortunately I have promised to be present at a large public dinner on that day.
Believe me,
Very truly yours,
E. LOVEL.

To a Lady, Inviting her to Luncheon.

5, PETERSHAM SQ., N.W.,
May 2nd, 18—.
DEAR MRS. CHURCHILL,
If disengaged, will you come to luncheon with us on Saturday next, at 2 o'clock? We shall be very pleased to see you.
Believe me,
Sincerely yours,
H. GRANT.

A Lady accepting an Invitation to Luncheon.

5, SEYMOUR STREET, N.W.,
May 3rd, 18—.
DEAR MRS. GRANT,
Many thanks for your kind invitation to luncheon on Saturday next. I have much pleasure in accepting it.
Sincerely yours,
M. CHURCHILL.

From a Lady, declining an Invitation to Luncheon.

5, SEYMOUR STREET, N.W.,
May 3rd, 18—.
DEAR MRS. GRANT,
I am sorry to say I shall not be able to come to luncheon with you on Saturday next, as I have promised to take my nieces to a morning performance at the Royal Theatre on that day, but I shall hope to see you in a few days, and will take my chance of finding you at home.
Believe me,
Sincerely yours,
M. CHURCHILL.

To a Gentleman, asking him to Luncheon.

5, CHICHESTER TERRACE, N.,
May 7th, 18—.

DEAR MR. BURNETT,

Will you come to luncheon here on Tuesday at 2 o'clock, if not otherwise engaged? You will meet an old friend of yours, so do come if you can.

Very truly yours,
E. BARNETT.

From a Gentleman, accepting an Invitation to Luncheon.

8, GEORGE STREET, W.,
May 8th, 18—.

DEAR MRS. BARNETT,

I shall be most happy to come to luncheon with you on Tuesday next. Your husband seems to have had a bad attack; I was glad to see him out again.

Very truly yours,
G. BURNETT.

From a Gentleman, refusing an Invitation to Luncheon.

8, GEORGE STREET, W.,
May 8th, 18—.

DEAR MRS. BARNETT,

I am sorry to say I cannot hope to have the pleasure of lunching with you on Saturday next, as I shall be particularly engaged all that afternoon with musketry practice. You must give my kind regards to the old friend you mentioned,— I have not an idea who it can be.

Very truly yours,
G. BURNETT.

To a Lady, Inviting her to Luncheon.

RIVERSIDE, KINGSTON,
July 7th, 18—.

DEAR MRS. LAWSON,

Will you and your party drive over here to luncheon next week? Would Thursday suit you if fine? Perhaps you will let me know in a day or two if I may expect you.

Sincerely yours,
H. WARREN.

Accepting an Invitation to Luncheon.

THE ELMS, WALTHAM,
July 8th, 18—.

DEAR MRS. WARREN,

It is very kind of you to ask us to drive over to luncheon next week. Thursday will suit us perfectly. We shall be a party of four, as Mr. and Mrs. Bond are leaving us to-morrow. My sister joins me in kind regards to yourself and Mr. Warren.

Believe me,
Sincerely yours,
G. LAWSON.

To a Lady, Inviting her to Luncheon.

5, CHICHESTER TERRACE, W.,
May 7th, 18—.

DEAR MISS CLARKE,

I shall be very pleased if you would come to luncheon with me next week. I will leave it for you to fix the day so as not to interfere with other engagements you may have made. I am only sorry your stay in town is to be so short.

Very sincerely yours,
E. BARNETT.

From a Lady, accepting an Invitation to Luncheon.

8, GREEN STREET, S.W.,
May 8th, 18—.

DEAR MRS. BARNETT,

I shall be very pleased to come to luncheon with you next week, and since you are kind enough to let me fix the day I think Friday will suit me best, as I shall be much engaged in the early part of the week.

Believe me,
Sincerely yours,
B. CLARKE.

To a Lady, asking her to Afternoon Tea.

5, CLARENCE GARDENS, S.W.,
Feb. 20th, 18—.

DEAR MRS. RANDOLPH,

I send you a card for an afternoon tea I purpose giving on the 2nd of March. I hope you may be able to come to it, and if you care to bring any friend of yours with you, pray do so.

Believe me,
Sincerely yours,
C. CONWAY.

From a Lady, accepting an Invitation to an Afternoon Tea.

5, RABY TERRACE, W.,
Feb. 21st, 18—.

DEAR MRS. CONWAY,

Many thanks for your card of invitation and kind note. I hope to be able to come to your tea next Friday and will bring my friend Miss Burch with me, as you are kind enough to say I may do so.

Sincerely yours,
H. RANDOLPH.

To a Lady, asking her to an Afternoon Tea.

THE DALE, HORNSEY, N.,
July 18th, 18—.

DEAR MRS. PALMER,

I expect several friends to afternoon tea on Saturday next, and hope to have a little good music. Perhaps you may be able to look in for half-an-hour, if so, I should be very pleased to see you.

Believe me,
Yours sincerely,
H. SHELFORD.

To a Young Lady, asking her to Sing at an Afternoon Tea.

> 9, THE AVENUE, NORWOOD,
> *Sept. 3rd,* 18—.

DEAR MISS GRAHAM,

I enclose a card for an afternoon tea I propose giving. I much hope you will be able to come to it. I should think it so kind of you if you would sing something for us ; several of my friends have promised their services for the occasion, and I expect we shall have some very good music.

> Believe me,
> Sincerely yours,
> G. BEAUMONT.

From a Lady, promising to Sing at an Afternoon Tea.

> 8, CEDAR VILLAS, NORWOOD,
> *Sept. 4th,* 18—.

DEAR MRS. BEAUMONT,

I shall be very happy to come to your tea on the 10th, and will bring one or two new songs with me which I think you will like.

> Sincerely yours,
> E. GRAHAM.

To a Lady, asking her to Tea.

> 5, CAMBRIDGE VILLAS, EALING,
> *Sept. 3rd,* 18—.

DEAR MISS WICKS,

If you have nothing better to do on Monday next, will you come to tea with me at five o'clock? I shall be very pleased if you would, I do not expect anyone but Mrs. Green. I was sorry not to see you when you called on Tuesday.

> Believe me,
> Truly yours,
> H. PRATT.

To a Gentleman, asking him to Recite at an Afternoon Tea.

5, THE TERRACE, PUTNEY,
March 7th, 18—,

DEAR MR. WHITE,

I enclose a card for my At Home next Tuesday afternoon, and hope so much you will be able to come to it. I wonder whether you would recite something during the afternoon? It would be most good-natured if you would allow yourself to be persuaded to do so.

Believe me,
Sincerely yours,
D. CAMPBELL.

To a Lady, inviting her to a Garden Party.

SYDNEY LODGE, SURBITON,
Aug. 10th, 18—.

DEAR MRS. KING,

We should be very pleased if you and any of your party would come over on Thursday next, the 13th instant, any time between three and seven o'clock to play lawn-tennis. We have only asked our immediate neighbours, but we expect some good players amongst them.

Sincerely yours,
L. MARSHAM.

Invitation to a Garden Party.

THE GROVE, WIMBLEDON,
June 28th, 18—.

DEAR MRS. PEAK,

I enclose you a card for a Garden Party we intend giving on the 12th of July. Pray bring any one who may be staying with you. I only hope we shall have a fine day, as everything depends upon the weather on these occasions. Believe me,

Yours very sincerely,
E. OSBORNE.

From a Lady, accepting an Invitation to a Garden Party.

THE CEDARS, WALTON,
Aug. 11th, 18—.

DEAR MRS. MARSHAM,

We shall be very happy to drive over on Thursday next to join your tennis party, weather permitting; an occasional shower would not prevent our coming, and only a thorough downfall would keep us away.

Sincerely yours,
E. KING.

To a Lady, inviting her to a Flower Show.

THE GRANGE, BASINGSTOKE,
Aug. 6th, 18—.

DEAR MISS FIELDING,

I hope you and your sister will be able to come to our village Flower Show on Wednesday the 13th instant. It is to be held in our grounds between three and seven o'clock, and we hope it will prove a success. There will also be exhibits of needlework by the school children, and the prizes are to be distributed at six o'clock by Sir George Blackwood.

Believe me,
Very sincerely yours,
E. LOVELL.

To a Lady, inviting her to a Picnic.

ROSENEATH, RYDE,
Aug. 3rd, 18—.

DEAR MISS BROOKE,

Mamma begs me to say that she will be very pleased if you and your brother will join our Picnic party on Saturday next, the 7th instant. We expect about fourteen people, and we are to start from   in two wagonettes at eleven o'clock. I trust you will be able to come, and that we shall have a very pleasant day.

Believe me,
Sincerely yours,
H. MEADOWS.

From a Lady, declining an Invitation to a Picnic.

SEA VIEW VILLA, SHANKLIN,
Aug. 4th, 18—.

DEAR MISS MEADOWS,

Thank you very much for your kind invitation which unfortunately we are unable to accept, as we are asked to an afternoon dance at Southsea on that day. My brother desires his kind regards and many regrets, in which I join.

Believe me,
Truly yours,
G. BROOKE.

To a Gentleman, inviting him to a Picnic.

ROSENEATH, RYDE,
Aug. 3rd, 18—.

DEAR MR. LUMLEY,

Can I persuade you to join our Picnic, on Saturday next? It is to be held at Copley Hill, but we are all to assemble here at 11 o'clock, and shall number between 14 and 15, including Miss Laws and Mrs. Unwin, both of whom you know.

Believe me,
Very truly yours,
H. MEADOWS.

From a Gentleman, accepting an Invitation to a Picnic.

5, PARK ROAD, SANDOWN,
Aug. 4th, 18—.

DEAR MRS. MEADOWS,

I shall be very happy to join your Picnic Party on Saturday next, and will be at your house at the hour named in your note.

Very truly yours,
W. LUMLEY.

From a Married Lady to another, inviting her to go to the Theatre.

18, GLOUCESTER STREET, S.W.,
November 8th, 18—.

DEAR MRS. BELL,

We have just had a box sent us at the Gaiety Theatre, for to-morrow evening, to see the new piece which

I hear is very good. I write to say how pleased I should be if you would join us, and either meet us at the theatre, or start with us from here, as most convenient to yourself.

Very truly yours,

E. MORLEY.

From a Lady, declining an Invitation to the Theatre.

8, WIMBORNE STREET, W.,
Nov. 9th, 18—.

DEAR MRS. MORLEY,

It would have been a great pleasure to have accepted your kind invitation to go with you to the theatre to-morrow evening, but I have unfortunately been confined to the house for some days with a bad cough, and dare not venture out in the night air.

Believe me with many thanks,

Very truly yours,

K. BELL.

From a Gentleman to a Young Lady, inviting her to go to the Theatre.

4, BRYANSTONE ST., S.W.,
November 10th, 18—.

DEAR MISS BARKER,

I think you said you would like to see the new piece at the Haymarket. If you will allow me I will endeavour to secure stalls for any evening next week on which you and your mother may be disengaged, and shall hope to have the pleasure of accompanying you.

Believe me,

Very truly yours,

H. HODGSON.

From a Lady to a Gentleman, accepting an Invitation to the Theatre.

8, TAVISTOCK PLACE, W.,
Nov. 11th, 18—.

DEAR MR. HODGSON,

My mother and I should much enjoy going to the theatre one day next week, and it is very kind of you to

offer to take stalls for us. I think Thursday would be the most convenient night if it suits you equally well.
Believe me, with kind regards from my mother,
Very sincerely yours,
A. BARKER.

To a Lady, asking her to a small Evening Party.

7, OAKFIELD TERRACE, S.W.,
Jan. 10th, 18—.

DEAR MISS BARTON,
Will you look in to-morrow at 9 o'clock and spend the evening with us? We mean to have a game of cards and a little music. I am sorry we cannot ask you to dinner, but I thought perhaps you might like to come to us in this friendly way.
Very truly yours,
H. DEANE.

To a Lady, inviting her to a Dance.

THE LAWN, RICHMOND,
Aug. 4th, 18—.

DEAR MRS. NEVILLE,
I think of giving a little dance on the 20th, and I hope you will all be able to come to it. It is quite an impromptu affair, not more pretentious than a carpet dance, but I trust your daughters will enjoy it nevertheless. Dancing will commence at half-past nine.
Believe me,
Very sincerely yours,
G. MANVERS.

From a Lady, refusing an Invitation to a Dance.

THE GREEN, HAMPTON COURT,
Aug. 5th, 18—.

DEAR MRS. MANVERS,
My daughters would have been delighted to have accepted the invitation to your dance, but we intend leaving home for Folkestone the end of this week, which will preclude their having the pleasure of doing so, much to their regret. I am sure your dance will be a great

success, and I am only so sorry that none of us can be present at it.

Believe me,
Very sincerely yours,
L. NEVILLE.

To a Young Lady, inviting her to a Dance.

8, BEDFORD GARDENS, W.,
Jan. 8th, 18—.

DEAR MISS MOORE,

Will you and your brother come to a little dance on the 20th, which Mamma is going to give in honour of my birthday? I hope you will be able to accept this invitation. We shall begin dancing soon after nine o'clock.

Believe me,
Yours affectionately,
LUCY SCOTT.

From a Young Lady, accepting an Invitation to a Dance.

19, BEAUFORT CRESCENT,
Jan. 9th, 18—.

DEAR MISS SCOTT,

Thank you very much for your kind invitation, which my brother and I have much pleasure in accepting.

With love, believe me,
Yours affectionately,
MABEL MOORE.

To a Gentleman, inviting him to a Dance.

8, TAVISTOCK CRESCENT, N.,
June 23rd, 18—.

DEAR MR. WILLIS,

I enclose a card for a dance we intend giving, as I have just heard that you were at home again. I hope you will be able to come, and if your cousin, Mr. Read, is staying with you, pray bring him, I shall be very pleased to see him.

Sincerely yours,
M. WOOD.

From a Gentleman, accepting an Invitation to a Dance.

102, MOUNT STREET,
June 24th, 18—.

DEAR MRS. WOOD,

Many thanks for your note and card of invitation, of which I shall certainly avail myself. My cousin started for Paris the beginning of this week, which will be sufficient excuse for his non-appearance.

Believe me, dear Mrs. Wood,
Very truly yours,
H. WILLIS.

To a Lady, inviting her on a Visit to Town.

10, BELGRAVE CRESCENT,
May 6th, 18—.

DEAR MISS ARMSTRONG,

I thought perhaps you would like to come up to town on a little visit, if so I should be very pleased if you would come to us next Monday, for a week or ten days. We will try to go to one or two concerts while you are with us, as I know music is a great treat to you, and my husband will perhaps take us to the theatre one night.

I shall hope to hear that I may expect you, and with love,

Believe me,
Affectionately yours,
E. COLLINS.

From a Lady, accepting an Invitation to stay in Town.

MANOR FARM, DORKING,
May 9th, 18—.

DEAR MRS. COLLINS,

Thank you very much for your kind invitation to stay with you next week. I am only too pleased to accept it, and hope to arrive at your house on Monday next, by the 5.30 train. I am quite looking forward to my little visit to you.

Believe me,
Affectionately yours,
E. ARMSTRONG.

To a Lady, asking her to pay a Country Visit.

THE HERMITAGE, READING,
May 11th, 18—.

DEAR MISS LONG,

I wonder if you would feel inclined for a little country air, if so perhaps you would like to run down to us for a few days. We are only an hour and a half from town as I think I told you. If you are able to come and will let me know what day to expect you, I would tell you the best train to take, and will send the pony-carriage to meet you. I need not say how pleased we should be to see you.

Believe me,
Sincerely yours,
C. MARTIN.

From a Lady, declining an Invitation to pay a Country Visit.

18, OXFORD CRESCENT, W.
May 12th, 18—.

DEAR MRS. MARTIN,

It would have given me much pleasure to have accepted your kind invitation to stay with you for a few days, but I have arranged to go down to Brighton on Friday next, with my sister-in-law, which will, I am sorry to say, prevent my coming to you just now. I always think the country is at its fairest this month, and I should have been so pleased to have paid you a little visit, could I have arranged it.

Believe me,
Very truly yours,
E. LONG.

To a Lady, inviting her to pay a Country Visit.

HOLLY LODGE, CHRISTCHURCH,
Aug. 7th, 18—.

DEAR MRS. EAST,

It would give us much pleasure if you would spend a few days with us on your way to the coast. I thought perhaps the 21st would suit you, if so I should be very happy to see you on that day. The country is looking lovely just now, and we will make some long excursions when you are here.

With kind remembrances from us all,

Believe me,

Sincerely yours,

E. PHILPOTT.

From a Lady, accepting a Country Invitation.

21, WEYMOUTH ST., W.,

Aug. 9th, 18—.

DEAR MRS. PHILPOTT,

I should much enjoy paying you a little visit as you so kindly propose. The 21st would suit me extremely well, and your invitation fits in charmingly with my plans, as I have taken rooms at Ryde from the 27th inst. I suppose Christchurch is your station and that the 3.30 train is a good one to come by. With kind regards to your party,

Sincerely yours,

J. G. EAST.

To a Lady, inviting her on a Visit to the Seaside.

PIER VILLA, RAMSGATE,

Sept. 8th, 18—.

DEAR MISS MOORE,

We have been here some three weeks and have enjoyed the change from town very much, the air is so bracing. Would you care to come down and spend a week with us? If so, it would give us much pleasure to see you. We shall be here at least a month longer, as far as I know at present. I can offer you a very comfortable room, and we have a fine view of the sea from our windows. Please remember me to your mother, and believe me,

Sincerely yours,

G. ROE.

From a Lady, accepting an Invitation to the Seaside conditionally.

8, LATIMER PLACE, N.W.,

Sept. 10th, 18—.

DEAR MRS. ROE,

It is very kind of you to ask me to stay with you at Ramsgate, and I should much like to accept your tempting invitation; but I am sorry to say at present I cannot leave home, as I have an invalid aunt requiring all my care. She has come up to town to consult her doctor. However, if you would renew your invitation in ten days' time, I think I might safely hope to have the pleasure of accepting it. With many thanks for thinking of me,

Believe me,
Very truly yours,
G. E. MOORE.

From a Lady, postponing a Dinner Party on account of a Death.

7, CHICHESTER GARDENS,
May 23rd, 18—.

DEAR MRS. HAMILTON,

I am sorry to say we cannot have the pleasure of seeing you and Mr. Hamilton at dinner to-morrow evening, on account of the death of my husband's sister, the sad intelligence of which only reached us this morning.

With many regrets,
Believe me,
Very sincerely yours,
E. MORTON.

From a Gentleman, excusing himself from keeping a Dinner Engagement on account of Indisposition.

192, EBURY ST., W.,
July 27th, 18—.

DEAR MRS. CLEMENTS,

I hope you will not pay yourself so bad a compliment as to imagine for a moment I am throwing you over, when I say that I am prevented, to my great regret, from having the pleasure of dining with you this evening. I have caught a severe cold which obliges me to stay in and take care of myself; my doctor even forbids my going to the office for an hour, so you will understand from this how genuine are these excuses. I am ever so sorry to be an absentee from such a pleasant party.

Believe me, very truly yours,
E. LOVEL.

From a Lady, excusing herself from keeping a Dinner Engagement on account of her Husband's Absence.

18, MARINE CRESCENT, BATH,
Dec. 14th, 18—.

DEAR MRS. NORTON,

I regret to say we are prevented having the pleasure of dining with you this evening, and I must ask you to kindly accept our excuses. My husband was telegraphed for this morning, and started by the 9.20 train for town, where I fear he will be detained several days.

Believe me,
Very truly yours,
C. WHITE.

From a Lady to a Gentleman, postponing a Dance.

8, TAVISTOCK TERRACE, W.,
June 28th, 18—.

DEAR MR. WILLIS,

I find that I am obliged to postpone my dance from the 1st to the 12th of July. I therefore renew my invitation for that date, and trust you will be able to accept it.

Sincerely yours,
M. WOOD.

From a Lady, postponing a Garden Party.

THE GROVE, WIMBLEDON,
July 3rd, 18—.

DEAR MRS. PEAK,

I am sorry to say I have been obliged to postpone my Garden Party from the 12th to the 28th instant, as I have had so many disappointments owing to there being two other garden parties in this neighbourhood fixed for the 12th, unto which many of my friends appear to be going.

I hope this change of date will not prevent your coming to us according to promise.

Believe me,
Very sincerely yours,
E. OSBORNE.

From a Lady, postponing a Friend's Visit to her on account of Illness in the Family.

HOLLY LODGE, CHRISTCHURCH,
August 12th, 18—.

DEAR MRS. EAST,

I am so sorry to have to ask you to postpone your visit to us for the present, but my little girl has been very unwell the last two days, and this morning the doctor tells me that she has a slight attack of measles.

It is very unfortunate, as we were much looking forward to your visit. However, I trust it is only a pleasure deferred, and that we may see you here before long.

Believe me, dear Mrs. East,

Very sincerely yours,

E. PHILPOTT.

CHAPTER XIII.

BUSINESS LETTERS.

From a Tenant to a Landlord, respecting Repairs.

CLAREMONT VILLAS, BARNES,
March 22nd, 18—.

DEAR SIR,

I shall be obliged, if you will send some one at once to examine the roof of this house, as the rain comes through in several places. I am sorry to say the pipes are also out of order, and require immediate attention to prevent further mischief.

I am, Sir,
Yours faithfully,
H. THOMAS.

Answer from a Landlord to a Tenant, respecting Repairs.

1, CARLTON ROAD, S.W.,
March 31st, 18—.

DEAR SIR,

I am in receipt of your letter of the 21st instant, and have desired Mr. Smith to have the necessary repairs done without delay; but as regards papering and painting the rooms you mention, I think it must be deferred until next year, when I will see what can be done. I must remind you that you were aware of the condition of the house when you took it, and that I made no promise respecting redecorations, as the rent paid by you does not warrant my incurring the outlay.

I am, Sir,
Yours obediently,
J. WILSON.

To H. THOMAS, Esq.

From a Tenant to a Landlord, complaining of Neglect.

ROSEMONT VILLA, KEW,
March 3rd, 18—.

DEAR SIR,

I called your attention some three weeks ago to the state of the drains of this house, but no notice has been taken of my letter. Unless you send some one at once to attend to this matter, I shall have no alternative but to apply to the Sanitary Inspector, and whatever he considers necessary I shall have done and charged to you.

I am, Sir,
Yours obediently,
J. WHITE.

To Mr. GREEN,

Answer from a Landlord to a Tenant, excusing Delay.

10, WOODSTOCK TERRACE, N.W.,
March 15th, 1883.

DEAR SIR,

I am sorry to hear that the repairs you require have not as yet been attended to. Owing to the late severe frost it is almost impossible to find plumbers for the amount of work required at the present moment; however I have desired my agent to send someone round to-morrow to ascertain the extent of the damage, and to put the job in hand at once.

I am, Sir,
Yours respectfully,
J. GREEN.

To J. WHITE, Esq.

From a Lady to a House Agent, making an Offer for a Furnished House.

SHEEN HOUSE, RICHMOND,
March 8th, 18—,

SIR,

I have been over No. 10, Bouverie Gardens, and should be glad to know if you think the owner would be ~osed to accept——guineas per month on consideration ~y being inclined to take the house for six months certain, providing the enclosed list of articles which I consider necessary are supplied.

Yours faithfully,

H. LOCKWOOD.

To MR. BROOK.

From a Lady to a House Agent, asking to put House on his Books.

72, BRUNSWICK TERRACE, BRIGHTON.
May 2nd, 18—.

SIR,

I shall be obliged if you will put this house on your books, as I wish to let it immediately if possible for two or three months. I enclose particulars of accommodation, rent required, etc.

Yours faithfully,

G. HALL.

From a Lady to a House Agent asking for Particulars of Houses.

SHEEN HOUSE, RICHMOND.
Aug. 4th, 18—.

SIR,

Have you any furnished houses on your books in the neighbourhood of —— at from 5 to $5\frac{1}{2}$ guineas per week? if so, will you send me the particulars of them, with orders to view? I should like to take a house for three months in that locality if I can find one to suit me.

Yours faithfully,

H. LOCKWOOD.

From a Lady to another respecting a Furnished House.

April 10th, 18—.

Mrs. King presents her compliments to Mrs. Johnson, she understands from her friend Mrs. Brooke, that Holly Lodge is to be let furnished, and she thinks from the description it would be very likely to suit her; perhaps Mrs. Johnson will let Mrs. King know when it will be convenient for her to see it.

4, CLARENDON GARDENS, S.W.

Answer from a Lady to another respecting a Furnished House.

April 11th, 18—.

Mrs. Johnson presents her compliments to Mrs King, and begs to thank her for her note respecting her house, but she has already received an offer for it, which she is disposed to accept. However should the matter fall through she will let Mrs. King know at once.

HOLLY LODGE, KINGSTON.

From a Clerk, asking for an Increase of Salary.

8, ST. JOHN'S TERRACE, CLAPHAM,
December 14th, 18—.

SIR,

Would you be disposed to make me a small increase of salary? as at my age and with my experience I feel that I ought to be earning more than I at present receive; perhaps when you take into consideration the fact that I have been in your employ over two years, you will not think this an unreasonable request, and be inclined to grant it. I need not say that in any case while I remain with you, my best energies will continue to be as they have hitherto been, devoted to your interests.

I am, Sir,
Yours obediently,
GEORGE LAWRENCE.

To H. SHEPHARD, Esq.

From a Clerk, thanking an Employer for an Increase of Salary.

8, St. John's Terrace, Clapham,
December 28th, 18—.

Sir,

I am very grateful for the increase of salary you have been good enough to promise me. It shall be my constant endeavour to continue to merit your confidence and goodwill and to give you every satisfaction in my power.

I am, Sir,

Yours obediently,

George Lawrence.

To Mr. H. Shephard.

To Employers, asking for a Holiday.

18, Beech Villas, Peckham,
Aug. 10th, 18—.

Gentlemen,

If quite convenient, would you allow me to take my usual holiday at the end of this month instead of in October? I should be most grateful for this concession if it could be made to fall in with your arrangements.

I am, Gentlemen,

Yours obediently,

Charles Halliday.

From a Clerk apologising to his Employers.

18, George Street, Islington,
Dec. 18th, 18—.

Sirs,

I very much regret the feeling of irritation which induced me to give you notice yesterday: will you permit me to apologise for so doing, and to ask you to allow me to recall it? I venture to make this request in the hope that my long, and I may say faithful services, will plead in my favour.

I am, Sirs,

Yours obediently,

To Messrs. Turner & Elsden.   Thomas Seely.

From a Commercial Traveller to his Employers.

THE RED LION HOTEL, CAMBRIDGE,
Dec. 2nd, 18—.

GENTLEMEN,

I beg to enclose a list of small orders which I have obtained from your old connection in this town. I am happy to say I have been able to extend it by adding two new firms to your list, and I believe in both instances you will find them very reliable. I proceed to-morrow to Shrewsbury, where I propose remaining two days; my address will be, White Hart Hotel, High Street.

I am, Gentlemen,

Yours obediently,

ROBERT TURPIN.

To MESSRS. CRAMPTON & NEAL.

Applying to a Firm to act as their Agent.

HIGH STREET, BURY ST. EDMUNDS,
October 9th, 18—.

GENTLEMEN,

It seems to me that there is a fair opening in this town for the sale of your new patent sewing machines, and I should be happy to act as your agent in this matter should you be disposed to entertain the idea. My premises are well suited for the purpose, being situated in our most popular thoroughfare, and as I do an extensive business in the ironmongery trade, I have great opportunities of introducing anything of special character to the notice of the neighbouring gentry and immediate townspeople. Mr. Rush, of North Street, and Mr. Brush, of South Street, would answer any inquiries relative to my standing in this town.

The question of commission on all sales is one for future consideration, subsequent to hearing from you in the affirmative.

I am, Gentlemen,

Yours obediently,

H. MILLER.

To MESSRS BIGMORE & CO.

From a Manufacturer to a Retail House.

THE ABERGATE CLOTH WORKS, DURHAM,
Jan. 24th, 18—.

DEAR SIRS,

I have recently established a cloth manufactory in this town, and herewith send a list of prices and samples of cloth. I am confident you will find that the best materials will be supplied at the lowest possible prices, and this I trust will induce you to open an account with me.

I am, Gentlemen,
Yours obediently,
ROBERT HEATH.

To MESSRS. GRIGG & ANGLE.

Complaining of Delay in Delivery of Foreign Goods.

21, FOREST STREET, CHEAPSIDE, E.C.,
April 17th, 18—.

DEAR SIRS,

I forwarded you on the 3rd instant an order for silks and velvets, with all particulars as to quality, price, pattern and colour. Up to the present moment I have not received the invoice of the same, or any intimation as to the order having been dispatched. Kindly wire the cause of delay, and date when goods will be to hand.

I am, Gentlemen,
Yours obediently,
G. KENT.

To MESSRS. DUBOIS & CIE.

From a Retail Tradesman to a Wholesale Firm.

17, HIGH STREET, GLOUCESTER,
April 3rd, 18—.

MESSRS. WHITE & JONES.

Gentlemen,

I have been recommended to your firm by Messrs. Saunders, of 26, St. Anne's Alley, and provided your prices meet my views, I should be glad to open an account with you for certain articles. I enclose a list of goods required. Will you oblige me with your prices for the same and the rate of discount or length of credit allowed?

I am, Gentlemen,
Yours obediently,
H. ARMSTRONG.

From a Wholesale Firm to a Retail Tradesman.

200, MINCING LANE, E.C.
April 4th, 18—.

DEAR SIR,

In reply to your favour of the 3rd instant, we beg to forward our printed list of prices. We are able to guarantee the quality of the goods should you be disposed to entrust us with your orders. We allow 5 per cent. discount on all cash payments, or the usual three months' credit.

We are, Sir,
Yours obediently,
WHITE & JONES.

From a Wholesale Firm to a Tradesman, asking for Payment of Account.

NEW WHARF, BERMONDSEY,
Jan. 2nd, 18—.

SIR,

We beg to call your attention to the fact that your account has not been settled this month according to promise, and further to request that you will favour us with a cheque for the same in the course of this week.

We are, Sir,
Yours obediently,
BRAKE & SMETHURST.

From a Creditor to a Tradesman, asking for Payment.

MEDWAY WORKS, BIRMINGHAM,
August 27th, 18—.

DEAR SIR,

I beg to remind you that your account still remains unsettled, and that it is now three months over-due. Should I not receive a remittance from you by Thursday next, I shall have no alternative but to place the matter in the hands of my solicitors.

I am, Sir,
Yours obediently,
H. DAVIS.

To MR. ALLEN.

From a Tradesman to a Creditor, asking for Time.

8, JAMES STREET, SHREWSBURY,
December 4th, 18—.

DEAR SIR,

May I ask your indulgence with regard to my over-due account, as owing to unforeseen circumstances I find it is not in my power to settle it under three months from this date. I think it best to solicit this favour frankly rather than to allow you to expect payment unfortunately not forthcoming. I need not say how much I regret this delay, which is nevertheless unavoidable.

I am, Sir,
Yours obediently,
H. ALLEN.

To H. DAVIS, Esq.

From a Tradesman to a Customer, requesting Payment.

18, NEW STREET, BIRMINGHAM,
Dec. 2nd, 18—.

SIR,

May I beg to call your attention to my outstanding account, and to ask if you will do me the favour to remit me a cheque for the same at your earliest convenience.

Yours obediently,
H. FOREST.

From a Wholesale Firm declining to give Credit.

66, BOROUGH ROAD, E.C.,
Jan. 7th, 18—,

SIR,

We beg to acknowledge your favour of the 3rd instant, and shall be happy to execute the order forwarded on receipt of your cheque for same.

It would not, we regret to say, answer our purpose to open a credit account with you.

We are, Sir,
Yours obediently,
PARKER & RANNS.

To MR. BRIGGS.

From a Wholesale Firm asking for References.

119, OLD JURY, E.C.,
May 6th, 18—.

DEAR SIR,

As you are desirous of opening an account with us, will you favour us with two references, as we have hitherto had no business transactions with you? In all cases when cash payments do not accompany the orders received from firms personally unknown to us, it is our rule to ask for references.

We are, Sir,
Yours obediently,
GRINDELL & MARSHALL.

To MR. G. TAYLOR.

To a Gentleman, soliciting a Confidential Opinion respecting a Firm.

8, BOROUGH ROAD, NEWCASTLE,
October 18th, 18—.

DEAR SIR,

I am about to engage in rather extensive transactions with the firm of Messrs. Bagley & Fordham, and as a matter of precaution I venture to ask if you can give me any information in the strictest confidence respecting their commercial position in your town, and the estimation in which they are held.

Trusting that if it is in your power you will so far oblige me,

I am, dear Sir,
Yours obediently,

To H. PERRY, Esq.   MARTIN SHELFORD.

Inquiries respecting the Pecuniary Position of Tradesman.

18, WHITEFRIARS ST., E.C.,
June 7th, 18—.

DEAR SIR,

Mr. Baker, of 17, High Street, Lowestoft, desires to open an account with our house, and has given your name as a reference. We should be glad to know if in your dealings with him you have found him punctual as to payments.

Yours obediently,
DUNN & MATHEWS.

To MR. PARKER.

Inquiries respecting the Pecuniary Position of a Tradesman.

18, WHITEFRIARS STREET, E.C.,
Jan. 9th, 18—.

DEAR SIRS,

Can you favour us with any information respecting the commercial standing in your town of Mr. Baker, of 17, High Street? If you have no personal knowledge of him, would you oblige us by making a few inquiries and informing us of the result? He is desirous of opening an account with us of rather an extensive character.

Yours obediently,
DUNN & MATHEWS.

To MESSRS. HARDWICKE & FLETCHER.

Favourable answer to Inquiries respecting the Position of a Tradesman.

6, WEST STREET, LOWESTOFT,
Jan. 12th, 18—.

DEAR SIRS,

In reply to your favour of the 9th instant, we beg to say our business relations with Mr. Baker have been hitherto most satisfactory, and we have a personal esteem for him as a man of thorough integrity.

We are,
Faithfully yours,
HARDWICKE & FLETCHER.

To MESSRS. DUNN & MATHEWS.

Unfavourable answer respecting the Position of a Tradesman.

5, ST. ANDREW'S STREET, LOWESTOFT,
Jan. 11th, 18—.

DEAR SIRS,

In reply to yours of the 9th instant, we beg to inform you that we have no personal knowledge of Mr. Baker; however, we have made several inquiries respecting him in reliable quarters, and cannot, we regret to say, learn anything in his favour.

We are, Gentlemen,
Yours obediently,
HARDWICKE & FLETCHER.

To MESSRS. DUNN & MATHEWS.

From a Firm, enclosing Account and Bill for Acceptance.

THE ROYAL CLOTH WORKS, BRADFORD,
Dec. 2nd, 18—.

DEAR SIR,

We beg to forward you the statement of your account up to present date, and with it enclose a bill for acceptance, which please return in due course.

Yours obediently,
HARDING & CLIFFORD.

To MR. PARSONS.

Respecting a Dishonoured Bill of Exchange.

14, VINCENT STREET, E.C.,
Jan. 4th, 18—.

SIR,

I beg to inform you that your bill of acceptance for £100 due 3rd instant has been returned to me through my bankers, it having been duly presented and dishonoured. Unless you are prepared to take it up in the course of to-morrow, defraying the necessary expenses of same, the usual proceedings to recover the amount will be at once instituted. The bill is now lying at Messrs. Wright & Co., Notary's office, 107, Southampton Street.

I am, Sir,
Yours obediently,
HENRY WADE.

To a Gentleman respecting a Bill of Exchange.

HEAVY TREE HOUSE, PUTNEY,
Jan. 9th, 18—.

DEAR BROWN,

I was induced to put my name to a bill for you on the clear understanding that the money would be forth-coming at the time named, and that I should hear nothing more about it. I yesterday received intimation from Mr. Schwab that it has been presented at your bankers as previously arranged but has not been met, and I have of course been compelled to pay it at great inconvenience to myself. You will have the goodness to attend to this matter at once, and I must say you had no right to let me in in this way.

Yours truly,
GEORGE MARTIN.

From a Member wishing to withdraw his Share in a Building Society.

7, HIGH STREET, WANDSWORTH,
Dec. 8th, 18—.

SIR,

I beg to give you notice (according to Rule XIV.) of withdrawal of my subscriptions to the Mutual Building

Society, and forward my book herewith, by which you will
see that the amount to my credit is £14 9s. 2d., I will
thank you to lay this letter before the Board, and to
forward me a cheque for the amount in due course.

Yours faithfully,
H. PARKER.

To a Solicitor, giving Notice to pay off a Mortgage.

ST. LEONARDS,
Jan. 13th, 18—.

To Mr. Lion,

DEAR SIR,

I beg to say that I have determined, by the advice
of my friends, to pay off the two existing mortgages on my
reversion, and will you therefore inform your clients of my
intention, and ask them if they will consent to take 3
months' interest in lieu of the required 6 months' notice,
as I am given to understand it is quite usual for mortgagees
to take their money back upon these terms. Will you
acquaint me with your clients' decision at your earliest convenience?

Believe me,
Faithfully yours,
CHARLOTTE STEBBING.

To a Solicitor respecting a Bill of Costs.

ST. LEONARDS,
Jan. 13th, 18—.

Mr. Lion,

DEAR SIR,

I enclose you a cheque for £25 6s. 8d., in full
discharge of all claims against me, including fee to
Actuary.

With regard to incurring further costs of any kind, I beg
to say that I do not intend doing so; neither do I wish
to take up your valuable time in correspondence at my
expense.

As I have said, I only require an answer from the mortgagees—yes or no—to my proposal, and I do not desire to enter into a correspondence on the subject.

                    I am, Sir,
                        Faithfully yours,
                            CHARLOTTE STEBBING.

From a Tradesman to a Firm respecting Returns.

                    102, OLD KENT ROAD,
                        Jan. 10th, 18—.

GENTLEMEN,

    Your statement is to hand.   Before sending you a cheque, I will thank you to correct the invoices of Dec. 9th and Jan. 12th last, on which days your carman took away and signed for 4 poles and 3 bags, and 5 bags and 3 poles respectively.   Please credit my account with these returns.

                    Yours faithfully,
                        J. ROBERTS.

From a Firm to a Customer respecting an Order.

                    28, BOROUGH ROAD,
                        November 20th, 18—.

DEAR SIR,

    We regret to say that we have been unable to procure the three castings to pattern.   We could make the same in about three days, price 28s. each.   Awaiting the favour of your order, which shall have our best attention,

                    We are, yours obediently,
                        SAUNDERS & Co.

From a Gentleman to his Tailor.

                    THE COMMON, BLACKHEATH,
                        Dec. 14th, 18—.

Mr. Brown,
    SIR,
        The coat you sent me down yesterday is a misfit in every way.   It is too large across the shoulders, tight

under the arms, narrow in the chest; the sleeves also are too short, and the collar is full of wrinkles. Considering that I was measured for it, and that it was subsequently tried on, there is no excuse for its fitting so badly. I have this morning returned it to you, and if the alterations are not made to my satisfaction, I shall of course decline to keep it.

I am, Sir,
Yours faithfully,
G. MOORE.

From a Gentleman to a Fishmonger.

17, ROSE TERRACE, MAIDA VALE,
July 24th, 18—.

SIR,

You undertook to supply me with first class fish at 6d. per head per day, for a family of six persons; but during the last fortnight the fish has fallen off both in quality and quantity; so much so, that I could obtain a better supply of fish from our local fishmonger at half the price. If you cannot undertake to send me fish as formerly, I shall consider my contract with you at an end, and must beg you to send your account up to present date.

Faithfully yours,
H. SHARP.

From a Gentleman to a House Furnisher, asking for Time in the Settlement of his Account.

HEATH VILLA, CLAPHAM RISE,
Feb. 16th, 18—.

Mr. Naples,

SIR,

I very much regret that I am unable to settle the whole of your account to-day; but I send you a cheque for £25 on account, and will endeavour to let you have the balance, £66 17s. 4d., on the 28th of next month. I shall feel greatly obliged by your allowing this amount to stand over until then, when you may depend upon receiving it.

Faithfully yours,
J. JACKSON.

From a Gentleman to a House Decorator, asking for an Estimate.

St. John's Sq., Chiswick,
April 23rd, 18—,

Mr. White,
Sir,

I wish to have the outside of this house painted down, and I should be obliged by your sending a responsible person to call on me respecting this matter, and to give me an estimate of the cost. I should also be glad to know if you can undertake to complete the work in the course of next week.

Faithfully yours,
G. Saunders.

From a Lady to a Coach Builder, asking for an Estimate.

April 24th, 18—.

Mrs. Mason wishes to have her pony-carriage repaired, painted, and re-lined, but would like to go to as little expense as possible. Will Messrs. Woodward therefore send her an estimate of the lowest possible price they could charge for the work she requires done? She will send the pony-carriage over to-morrow morning, and should it not be worth the outlay, perhaps Messrs. Woodward would frankly say so.

Tiverton Villa, Mitcham.

From a Lady, complaining of a Mistake in an Account.

May 6th, 18—.

Mrs. Thompson finds there is a small mistake in Mr. Wilson's account, 7 yards of velveteen having been charged for which were returned by her on April 27th, when she explained that the colour did not match the pattern forwarded to Mr. Wilson. If he will deduct this item from the enclosed account, Mrs. Thompson will settle it at once.

5, Cambridge Villas, Surbiton.

M

From a Lady to a Dressmaker postponing the Payment of an Account.

Jan. 18th, 18—.

MRS. FULBOURN is sorry she cannot send Miss Willis a cheque by return as requested, but hopes to be able to do so in the course of the next ten days. She had not forgotten Miss Willis' account, and is only sorry that she has been obliged to keep her waiting for it so long a time.

CLARENCE VILLA, DENMARK HILL.

From a Lady to a Dressmaker.

June 8th, 18—.

MRS. ROSE has received Miss Smart's account, and is sorry to find that it is considerably higher than she had expected. She will call and see Miss Smart in the course of the week respecting two or three items which require explanation.

17, ST. PETER'S TERRACE, HAMMERSMITH.

From a Lady, asking for Patterns.

April 8th, 18—.

MISS ALLEN would be obliged if Messrs. Watt & Roberts would forward her a few patterns of Prune Cashmere, from 2s. 6d. to 3s. per yard, also patterns of cambrics at about 9d. per yard; dark colours preferred.

1, GOLDFIELD VILLAS, NEWMARKET.

CHAPTER XIV.

THE RECEIVED FORMS FOR COMMENCING, CONCLUDING, AND ADDRESSING LETTERS.

THE SOVEREIGN.

To the Queen.

Commencement of Letter Officially.

Madam,
    May it please your Majesty, *or,*
    Lord P. presents his humble duty to your Majesty.

Conclusion.

I have the honour to remain your Majesty's most faithful subject and dutiful servant.

Superscription of Envelope.

To Her Most Gracious Majesty Queen Victoria.

Commencement of Letter Socially.

Dear and Honoured Madam.

Conclusion.

I have the honour to remain,
    Your Majesty's most dutiful and humble servant.

Superscription of Envelope as above.

To a Prince of the Blood Royal.

Commencement of Letter Officially.

Sir,
    May it please your Royal Highness.

Conclusion.

I have the honour to remain, Sir,
Your Royal Highness' most humble and dutiful servant.

Superscription of Envelope.

To His Royal Highness the Prince of Wales.
Marlborough House, S.W.

Commencement of Letter Socially.

Dear Sir.

Conclusion.

Your Royal Highness' most humble and obedient servant.

Superscription of Envelope as above.

To a Princess of the Blood Royal.

Commencement of Letter Officially.

Madam,
May it please your Royal Highness.

Conclusion.

I have the honour to remain, Madam,
Your Royal Highness' most humble and dutiful servant.

Superscription of Envelope.

To Her Royal Highness the Princess of Wales.
Marlborough House, S.W.

Commencement of Letter Socially.

Dear Madam.

Conclusion.

Your Royal Highness' most humble and obedient servant.

Superscription of Envelope as above.

TO MEMBERS OF THE ARISTOCRACY.

To a Duke.

Commencement of Letter Officially.

My Lord Duke,
  May it please your Grace.

Conclusion.

I have the honour to be,
  Your Grace's most obedient and humble servant.

Superscription of Envelope.

To His Grace The Duke of Wiltshire, K.G.*

Commencement of Letter Socially.

My dear Lord Duke, *or,*
My dear Duke, *or,*
Dear Duke of Wiltshire.

Conclusion.

Believe me, dear Duke,
      Your Grace's very faithfully, *or,*
  I have the honour to remain,
      Your Grace's most obediently.

Superscription of Envelope.

To His Grace The Duke of Wiltshire, K.G., *or,*
To The Duke of Wiltshire, K.G.

To a Duchess.

Commencement of Letter Officially.

Madam,
  May it please your Grace, *or,*
  Will your Grace.

Conclusion.

I have the honour to remain,
  Your Grace's most humble and obedient servant.

Superscription of Envelope.

To Her Grace The Duchess of Wiltshire.

* K.G. when a Knight of the Garter ; K.T. when a Knight of the Thistle.

To a Dowager.

To Her Grace The Dowager Duchess of Wiltshire, *or*,
To Her Grace Elizabeth Duchess of Wiltshire.

Commencement of Letter Socially.

Mr. Chamberlain ventures to ask the Duchess of Wilt-
shire, if Her Grace will kindly consent to, *or*,
Dear Duchess of Wiltshire, *or*,
Dear Duchess.

Conclusion.

I have the honour to remain,
　　　Your Grace's very truly, *or*,
Believe me, dear Duchess,
　　　Yours very sincerely.

Superscription of Envelope.

To Her Grace The Duchess of Wiltshire.
To The Duchess of Wiltshire.

To a Marquis.

Commencement of Letter Officially.

My Lord Marquis.

Conclusion.

I have the honour to be,
　　　Your Lordship's humble and obedient servant.

Superscription of Envelope.

To The Most Noble The Marquis of Sussex.

Commencement of Letter Socially.

My dear Lord, *or*,
Dear Lord Sussex, *or*,
* Dear Sussex.

Superscription of Envelope.

To The Marquis of Sussex.

---

* The surname Sussex without the title is only used thus, when a
man is the writer.

To a Marchioness.

Commencement of Letter Officially.

Madam.

Conclusion.

I have the honour to remain,
Your Ladyship's most humble and obedient servant.

Superscription of Envelope.

To The Most Noble The Marchioness of Sussex.

Commencement of Letter Socially.

Dear Lady Sussex.

Conclusion.

Believe me, dear Lady Sussex,
Very sincerely yours, *or,*
Very truly yours.

Superscription of Envelope.

To The Marchioness of Sussex.

To a Dowager.

To The Dowager Marchioness of Sussex, *or,*
To Maria Marchioness of Sussex.

To an Earl.

Commencement of Letter Officially.

My Lord.

Conclusion.

I have the honour to remain,
Your Lordship's most humble and obdient servant.

Superscription of Envelope.

To The Right Honourable The Earl of Kent.

Commencement of Letter Socially.

My dear Lord *or,*
Dear Lord Kent, *or,*
Dear Kent.

Conclusion.

Believe me, my dear Lord,
    Very faithfully yours, *or,*
Believe me, dear Lord Kent,
    Very sincerely yours, *or,*
I am, dear Kent,
    Very truly yours.

Superscription of Envelope.

To The Earl of Kent.

To a Countess.

Commencement of Letter Officially.

Madam.

Conclusion.

I have the honour to remain,
    Your Ladyship's most humble and obedient servant.

Superscription of Envelope.

To The Right Honourable The Countess of Kent.

Commencement of Letter Socially.

Dear Lady Kent.

Conclusion.

Believe me, dear Lady Kent,
        Very sincerely yours, *or,*
        Very faithfully yours.

Superscription of Envelope.

To The Countess of Kent.

To a Viscount.

Commencement of Letter Officially.

My Lord.

Conclusion.

I have the honour to remain,
    Your Lordship's most humble and obedient servant.

Superscription of Envelope.

To The Right Honourable The Viscount Surrey.

Commencement of Letter Socially.

My dear Lord, *or,*
Dear Lord Surrey, *or,*
Dear Surrey.

Conclusion.

I am, my dear Lord,
Yours very faithfully, *or,*
I am, dear Lord Surrey,
Yours very sincerely, *or,*
I am, dear Surrey,
Very truly yours.

Superscription of Envelope.

To The Viscount Surrey.

To a Viscountess.

Commencement of Letter Officially.

Madam.

Conclusion.

I have the honour to remain,
Your Ladyship's most humble and obedient servant.

Superscription of Envelope.

To The Right Honourable The Viscountess Surrey.

Commencement of Letter Socially.

Dear Lady Surrey.

Conclusion.

Believe me, dear Lady Surrey,
Very faithfully yours, *or,*
Believe me, dear Lady Surrey,
Very sincerely yours.

Superscription of Envelope.

To The Viscountess Surrey.

To a Baron.

Commencement of Letter Officially.

My Lord.

Conclusion.

I have the honour to remain,
Your Lordship's most humble and obedient servant.

Superscription of Envelope.

To The Right Honourable The Baron Cumberland.

Commencement of Letter Socially.

My dear Lord, *or,*
Dear Lord Cumberland, *or,*
Dear Cumberland.

Conclusion.

I am, my dear Lord,
Very faithfully yours, *or,*
Believe me, dear Lord Cumberland,
Very truly yours, *or,*
I am, dear Cumberland,
Very truly yours.

Superscription of Envelope.

To The Lord Cumberland.

To a Baroness.

Commencement of Letter Officially.

Madam.

Conclusion.

I have the honour to remain,
Your Ladyship's most humble and obedient servant.

Superscription of Envelope.

To The Right Honourable The Baroness Cumberland.

Commencement of Letter Socially.

Dear Lady Cumberland.

Conclusion.

Believe me, dear Lady Cumberland,
Very faithfully yours, *or,*
Very sincerely yours.

Superscription of Envelope.

To The Lady Cumberland.

In addressing the widow of a nobleman by letter the words "The Dowager" or the Christian name of the lady precede the title as she may please to adopt: thus,

Officially.

The Right Honourable The Dowager Baroness Cumberland, *or,*
The Right Honourable Elizabeth Baroness Cumberland.

Socially.

The Dowager Lady Cumberland, *or,*
Elizabeth, Lady Cumberland.

To the Younger Son of a Duke or Marquis.

Commencement of Letter Officially.

My Lord.

Conclusion.

I have the honour to remain,
Your Lordship's most humble and obedient servant.

Superscription of Envelope.

To The Right Honourable The Lord John Bath.

Commencement of Letter Socially.

My dear Lord, *or,*
Dear Lord John Bath, *or,*
Dear Lord John, *or,*
Dear Bath.

Conclusion.

Believe me, my dear Lord, *or,*
Believe me, dear Lord John,
Very faithfully yours, *or,*
Very truly yours.

Superscription of Envelope.

To The Lord John Bath.*

To the Wife of a Younger Son of a Duke or Marquis.

Commencement of Letter officially.

Madam.

Conclusion.

I have the honour to remain,
Your Ladyship's most humble and obedient servant.

Superscription of Envelope.

To The Right Honourable The Lady John Bath.

Commencement of Letter Socially.

Dear Lady John Bath, *or,*
Dear Lady John.

Conclusion.

Believe me, dear Lady John Bath, *or,*
Dear Lady John,
Faithfully yours, *or,*
Sincerely yours.

Superscription of Envelope.

To The Lady John Bath.

To a Daughter of a Duke, a Marquis, or an Earl.

Commencement of Letter Officially.

Madam.

Conclusion.

I have the honour to remain,
Your Ladyship's most humble and obedient servant.

Superscription of Envelope.

To The Right Honourable The Lady Mary Bath.

---

* When the sons of peers are members of Parliament, the letters M.P
'ollow the title officially and socially. Thus—-The Lord John Bath, M.P

Commencement of Letter Socially.

Dear Lady Mary Bath, *or,*
Dear Lady Mary.

Conclusion.

Believe me, dear Lady Mary,
     Very faithfully yours, *or,*
     Very truly yours.

Superscription of Envelope.

To The Lady Mary Bath.

To the Younger Son of an Earl, Viscount, or a Baron.

Commencement of Letter Officially.

Sir, *or,*
Dear Sir.

Conclusion.

I have the honour to be, Sir,
     Your most obedient servant.

Superscription of Envelope.

To The Honble. Charles Cumberland.

Commencement of Letter Socially.

Dear Mr. Cumberland, *or,*
Dear Cumberland.

Conclusion.

Believe me, dear Mr. Cumberland, *or,*
     dear Cumberland,
          Very truly yours, *or,*
          Very faithfully yours.

Superscription of Envelope as above.

**To the Wife of a Younger Son of an Earl, or the Son
of a Viscount or Baron.**

Commencement of Letter Officially.

Madam.

Conclusion.

I have the honour to remain, Madam,
Your humble and obedient servant.

Superscription of Envelope.

To The Honble. Mrs. Cumberland.

Commencement of Letter Socially.

Dear Mrs. Cumberland.

Conclusion.

Believe me, dear Mrs. Cumberland,
Faithfully yours, *or,*
Sincerely yours.

Superscription of Envelope as above.

To the Daughter of a Viscount or Baron.

Commencement of Letter Officially.

Madam.

Conclusion.

I have the honour to be, Madam,
Your humble and obedient servant.

Superscription of Envelope.

The Eldest Daughter.

To The Honble. Miss Cumberland.

A Younger Daughter.

To The Honble. Evelyn Cumberland.*

Commencement of Letter Socially.

Dear Miss Cumberland.

Conclusion.

Believe me, dear Miss Cumberland,
Faithfully yours, *or,*
Sincerely yours.

Superscription of Envelope as above.

* The daughters of Peers retain their rank when married to the younger
son of a Poer, or to a Baronet or Commoner.

To a Baronet.

Commencement of Letter Officially.

Sir.

Conclusion.

I have the honour to remain, Sir,
Your humble and obedient servant.
To Sir John Westmoreland.

Superscription of Envelope.

To Sir John Westmoreland, Bart.*

Commencement of Letter Socially.

Dear Sir John Westmoreland, *or,*
Dear Sir John, *or,*
Dear Westmoreland.

Conclusion.

Believe me, dear Sir John Westmoreland, *or,*
dear Sir John, *or,*
dear Westmoreland,
Faithfully yours, *or,*
Sincerely yours.

Superscription of Envelope as above.

To the Wife of a Baronet.

Commencement of Letter Officially.

Madam.

Conclusion.

I have the honour to remain,
Your Ladyship's humble and obedient servant.

Superscription of Envelope.

To Lady Westmoreland.

Commencement of Letter Socially.

Dear Lady Westmoreland.

* When a Baronet is a member of Parliament the letters M.P. follow
the title both officially and socially. Thus—
Sir John Westmoreland, Bart., M.P.

Conclusion.

Believe me, dear Lady Westmoreland,
Faithfully yours, *or,*
Sincerely yours.

Superscription of Envelope as above

To a Knight

Commencement of Letter Officially.

Sir.

Conclusion.

I have the honour to remain, Sir,
Faithfully yours.
To Sir George Essex.

Superscription of Envelope.

To Sir George Essex, K.C.B., *or* K.C.M.G., *or* K.C.S.I.,
according to Order of Knighthood.

Commencement of Letter Socially.

Dear Sir George Essex, *or,*
Dear Sir George, *or,*
Dear Essex.

Conclusion.

Faithfully yours, *or,*
Sincerely yours.

Superscription of Envelope as above.

To the Wife of a Knight.

Commencement of Letter Officially.

Madam.

Conclusion.

I have the honour to remain,
Your Ladyship's humble and obedient servant.

Superscription of Envelope.

To Lady Essex.

Commencement of Letter Socially.

Dear Lady Essex.

Conclusion.

Believe me,

Faithfully yours, *or,*
Sincerely yours.

Superscription of Envelope as above.

To an Esquire.

Commencement of Letter Officially.

Sir, *or,*
Dear Sir.

Conclusion.

I have the honour to be, Sir,
Your obedient servant.

Superscription of Envelope.

To George Cole, Esquire.

If a Member of Parliament.

To George Cole, Esquire, M.P.

Commencement of Letter Socially.

Dear Mr. Cole, *or,*
Dear Cole.

Conclusion.

Faithfully yours, *or,*
Sincerely yours.

Superscription of Envelope as above.

To the Wife of an Esquire.

Commencement of Letter Officially.

Madam.

Conclusion.

I have the honour to be, Madam,
Your obedient servant.

Commencement of Letter Socially.
Dear Mrs. Cole.

Conclusion.
Faithfully yours, *or,*
Sincerely yours.

Superscription of Envelope.
To Mrs. Cole.

THE CLERGY.

To an Archbishop.

Commencement of Letter Officially.
My Lord Archbishop,
May it please your Grace.

Conclusion.
I remain, my Lord Archbishop,
Your Grace's most humble and obedient servant.

Superscription of Envelope.
The Most Rev. His Grace The Lord Archbishop of——

Commencement of Letter Socially.
My dear Lord, *or;*
My dear Lord Archbishop.

Conclusion.
I have the honour to remain,
My dear Lord Archbishop,
Your Grace's very faithfully, *or,*
Your Grace's very truly.

Superscription of Envelope as above. *

To a Bishop.

Commencement of Letter Officially.
My Lord.

* The Archbishop of Armagh is addressed as The Most Rev. His Grace the Lord Primate of Ireland.

Conclusion.

I have the honour to remain,
Your Lordship's humble and obedient servant.

Superscription of Envelope.

To the Right Rev. the Lord Bishop of Cambridge.

Commencement of Letter Socially.

My dear Lord, *or,*
My dear Lord Bishop.

Conclusion.

I have the honour to remain,
My dear Lord,
Faithfully yours, *or,*
Truly yours.

*Superscription of Envelope as above.**

To a Dean.

Commencement of Letter Officially.

Reverend Sir.

Commencement of Letter Socially.

Dear and Reverend Sir, *or,*
Dear Mr. Dean, *or,*
Dear Dean.

Superscription of Envelope.

To the Very Rev. the Dean of Kensington.

To an Archdeacon.

Commencement of Letter Officially.

Venerable Sir.

---

* Bishops Suffragan, Scotch Bishops, and Irish Bishops are addressed respectively as "Right Rev. Sir," with the exception of the Irish Bishops consecrated previous to 1868, who are addressed as are English Bishops and the Bishop of Meath. Colonial Bishops are addressed as are the Bishops of English sees.

Commencement of Letter Socially.
Dear Mr. Archdeacon, *or,*
Dear Archdeacon.

Superscription of Envelope.
To the Ven. Archdeacon of Bradford, *or,*
The Ven. the Archdeacon Bird.

To a Canon.

Commencement of Letter Officially.
Reverend Sir.

Commencement of Letter Socially.
Dear Canon Barnett.

Superscription of Envelope.
To the Rev. Canon Barnett.

To a Rector, Vicar, or Curate.

Commencement of Letter Officially.
Reverend Sir.

Commencement of Letter Socially.
Dear Mr. Wright.

Superscription of Envelope.
To the Rev. James Wright. D.D.*

* When a clergyman is the son of a Duke, or a Peer, his title follows his clerical title. Thus—
The Rev. Lord John Tryon.
Or in the case of a Baronet being in Holy Orders, thus—
The Rev. Sir Robert Hervey, Bart.
The right of dissenting ministers to the title of Reverend is often accorded them, but the proper style of address is—
Mr. James Fairburn,
Minister of Park Chapel.

THE ARMY.

To a General, Colonel, Major, Captain, or Lieutenant.

Commencement of Letter Officially.

Sir.

Commencement of Letter Socially.

Dear Gen. Green,
Dear Col. White,
Dear Major Black,
Dear Capt. Browne,
Dear Mr. Robinson.

Superscription of Envelope according to the rank of the Officer. Thus—

To Lieutenant-General White.
To Major-General White, *or,*
General White.*
To Colonel White.
To Major Black.
To Capt. Browne.
To H. Robinson, Esq.

THE NAVY.

To an Admiral, Captain, or Lieutenant.

Commencement of Letter Officially.

Sir.

Commencement of Letter Socially.

Dear Admiral Stone,
Dear Captain Broome.
Dear Mr. Jones.

* When writing officially, letters relating to orders of merit or orders of knighthood are in use, but not so when writing socially, save in the case of a K.C.B. when they would follow the name thus—
General Sir Henry Green, K.C.B.
When an officer is the son of a Peer, his title follows the military title thus—
Colonel the Honourable James White.

Superscription of Envelope according to rank, either,
Vice-Admiral, Rear-Admiral, *or,*
Admiral Stone.

To a Captain.

Capt. Broome, R.N., H.M.S. "Vulture."

To a Lieutenant.

H. Jones, Esqre. H.M.S. "Tyne."

THE BAR.

To the Lord Chancellor.

Commencement of Letter Officially.

My Lord.

Conclusion.

I have the honour to remain,
 Your Lordship's humble and obedient servant.

Commencement of Letter Socially.

My dear Lord, *or,*
Dear Lord Salter.

Superscription of Envelope Officially.

To the Rt. Hon. the Lord High Chancellor of Great
 Britain.

Socially.

To the Lord Chancellor the Earl of Salter, *or,*
According to rank.

To the Lord Chief Justice.

Commencement of Letter Officially.

My Lord.

Superscription of Envelope.
To the Lord Chief Justice of England.

Commencement of Letter Socially, according to individual rank.

To the Master of the Rolls.

Commencement of Letter Officially.
Sir.

Commencement of Letter Socially.
Dear Master of The Rolls.

Superscription of Envelope.
The Right Honourable Sir J. Robinson.
The Master of the Rolls.

To a Lord Justice of Appeal.

Commencement of Letter Officially.
My Lord Justice, *or,*
Sir.

Commencement of Letter Socially.
Dear Lord Justice.

Superscription of Envelope.
To the Right Hon. the Lord Justice Whitburn.

To the Solicitor-General.

Commencement of Letter Officially.
Sir.

Superscription of Envelope.
To the Right Honourable Sir James Pocock.
Solicitor-General, Q.C.

To the Attorney-General.

Commencement of Letter Officially.
Sir.

Superscription of Envelope.
To the Right Honourable Sir Henry Hunt.
Attorney-General. Q.C.

To a Queen's Counsel.

Commencement of Letter Officially.

Sir.

Superscription of Envelope.

To Charles Bullar, Esq., Q.C.,

To a Justice of the Queen's Bench Division.

Commencement of Letter Officially.

Sir.

Superscription of Envelope.

To the Honourable Sir Henry Pearson,
    Judge of the Queen's Bench Division, *or*,
To the Honourable Mr. Justice Pearson.

To a Vice-Chancellor.

Commencement of Letter Officially.

Sir.

Superscription of Envelope.

To the Honourable Sir Henry Cook, *or*,
To The Vice-Chancellor Sir Henry Cook.

To a Puisne Judge.

Commencement of Letter Officially.

Sir.

Superscription of Envelope.

To the Honourable Mr. Justice Ford.

THE MEDICAL PROFESSION.

To a Baronet.

Commencement of Letter Officially.

Sir.

Commencement of Letter Socially.
Dear Sir, *or,*
Dear Sir George King.
Superscription of Envelope.
To Sir George King, Bart., M.D.

To a Knight.
Commencement of Letter Officially.
Sir.
Commencement of Letter Socially.
Dear Sir, *or,*
Dear Sir Henry Payne.
Superscription of Envelope.
To Sir Henry Payne, K.M.G., M.D.

To a Doctor of Medicine.
Commencement of Letter Officially.
Sir.
Commencement of Letter Socially.
Dear Dr. Brown.
Superscription of Envelope.
W. Brown, Esqre. M.D.*

To a Medical Gentleman other than the above.
Commencement of Letter Officially.
Sir.
Commencement of Letter Socially.
Dear Sir, *or,*
Dear Mr. Turner.
Superscription of Envelope.
To Edward Turner, Esqre.

* If a member of the Royal College of Physicians, or of the Royal College of Surgeons, the letters F.R.C.P. or F.R.C.S. are added when writing officially.

THE GOVERNMENT.

To a Secretary of State.

Commencement of Letter Officially.

My Lord, *or,*
Sir, according to rank.

Conclusion.

I have the honour to be your Lordship's most humble
and obedient servant, *or,*
I have the honour to be, Sir, your obedient servant.

Superscription of Envelope.

To the Right Honourable the Earl of ——,
    Principal Secretary of State for Home Affairs : *or,*
To the Right Honourable the Earl of ——,
    Principal Secretary of State for the Colonies : *or,*
To the Right Honourable —— ——, M.P.,
    Secretary of State for War.

To the First Lord of the Admiralty.

Commencement of Letter Officially.

My Lord, *or,*
Sir, according to rank.

Superscription of Envelope.

To the Right Honourable —— ——,
    First Lord Commissioner of the Admiralty.

To the First Lord of the Treasury.

Commencement of Letter Officially.

My Lord, *or,*
Sir, according to rank.

Superscription of Envelope.

To the Right Honourable —— ——,
    First Lord of the Treasury,
    Prime Minister and Chancellor of the Exchequer.

To the President of the Board of Trade.

Commencement of Letter Officially.

Sir.

Superscription of Envelope.

The Right Honourable —— ——, M.P.
President of the Board of Trade.

To an English Ambassador at a Foreign Court.

Commencement of Letter Officially.

My Lord, *or,*
Sir, according to rank.

Superscription of Envelope.

To His Excellency the Right Honourable Sir George
—— , K.C.B.
Her Britannic Majesty's Ambassador
Extraordinary and Plenipotentiary at the Court
of ——.

To a Consul.

Commencement of Letter Officially.

Sir.

Superscription of Envelope.

To —— ——, Esqre.,
Her Majesty's Britannic Consul at ——.

To the Postmaster-General.

Commencement of Letter Officially.

My Lord, *or,*
Sir, according to rank.

Superscription of Envelope.

To the Right Honourable —— ——, M.P.
Postmaster-General.

To the Lord Chamberlain.

Commencement of Letter Officially.

My Lord.

Superscription of Envelope.

To the Right Honourable the Earl of ——,
        Lord Chamberlain.

To the Lord-Lieutenant of Ireland.

Commencement of Letter Officially.

My Lord Duke, *or,*
My Lord, according to rank.
May it please Your Grace, *or,*
May it please Your Excellency.

Superscription of Envelope.

To His Grace the Duke of ——,
        Lord-Lieutenant of Ireland, *or,*
To His Excellency the Right Honourable Earl of ——,
        Lord-Lieutenant of Ireland.

To the Wife of the Lord-Lieutenant of Ireland.

Commencement of Letter Officially.

Madam.
May it please Your Grace, *or,*
May it please Your Excellency, according to rank.

Superscription of Envelope.

To Her Grace the Duchess of ——, *or*
To Her Excellency the Countess of ——.

To the Governor of a Colony.

Commencement of Letter Officially.

My Lord, *or,*
Sir, according to rank.

Superscription of Envelope.
To His Excellency Sir George ——, K.C.M.G.,
Governor of ——.

The Lord Mayor.

Commencement of Letter Officially.

My Lord.

Superscription of Envelope.
To the Right Honourable the Lord Mayor.

To the Lady Mayoress.

Commencement of Letter Officially.

Madam.

Conclusion.
I have the honour to remain,
Your Ladyship's
Humble and obedient servant,

Superscription of Envelope.
To the Right Honourable the Lady Mayoress.

To a Mayor.

Commencement of Letter Officially.

Sir.

Superscription of Envelope.
To the Rt. Worshipful the Mayor of ——.

CHAPTER XV.

FORMS RELATING TO BUSINESS TRANSACTIONS.

An Agreement for a Lease for a Certain Period.

AN AGREEMENT made this twenty-seventh day November one thousand eight hundred and eighty three BETWEEN JOHN WILLIAM EVERETT of Guildford in the County of Surrey Mill owner of the one part and SUSAN POTTER of number 17 Gloucester Road London Spinster of the other part as follows   The said John William Everett agrees to let, and the said Susan Potter agrees to take ALL THAT messuage or dwelling house and premises known as number 17 Gloucester Road London aforesaid Together with all easements and appurtenances thereto belonging for the term of FIVE YEARS (determinable nevertheless as hereinafter mentioned) from the twenty ninth day of September last at the yearly rent of one hundred and ten pounds clear of all existing and future taxes rates and outgoings (Landlord's property tax only excepted) to be payable by four equal payments on the twenty fifth day of December the twenty fifth day of March the twenty fourth day of June and the twenty ninth day of September in every year the first of such payments to be made on the twenty fifth day of December next.   The said John William Everett his heirs or assigns will on the request of the said Susan Potter her executors administrators or authorized assigns execute a proper lease of the said premises to the said Susan Potter her executors administrators or authorized assigns for the term and at the rent aforesaid to be payable as aforesaid.   The said lease shall contain covenants on the part of the said Susan Potter her executors administrators and authorized assigns for payment of the said net yearly rent of one hundred and ten pounds on the days and in manner aforesaid And for payment of all existing and future taxes rates and outgoings (Landlord's property tax only excepted) And to keep the inside of the said premises in good and sufficient condition and repair (accidents by fire only excepted) and in such good and sufficient condition and repair (except as aforesaid) to deliver up the same premises with all new fixtures and other additions to the said John William Everett his heirs or assigns at the expiration or other sooner determination of the said term And that it shall be lawful for the said John William Everett his heirs or assigns at any time or times to enter upon the said premises to view the condition thereof and of all defects and wants of reparation of the inside thereof to give notice in writing to the said Susan Potter her executors administrators or authorized assigns And that she the said Susan Potter her executors administrators or authorized assigns will within three months from the date of such notice being given make good and repair all such defects and wants of reparation as aforesaid And not to assign or underlet the said premises without license in writing from the said John William Everett his heirs or assigns And not to carry on or permit to be carried on upon the said premises any trade or business whatsoever but use and keep the same as a private dwellinghouse only And not to permit any auction sale to be held or take place on the said premises The said lease shall also contain a proviso for re-entry by the said John William Everett his heirs or assigns on non-payment of the said yearly rent of one hundred and ten pounds or any part thereof for twenty one days next after any of the said days on which the same or any part thereof shall become due and whether the same shall have been legally demanded or not or on the breach of any of the covenants by the lessee in the said lease to be contained. And also a proviso for determination of the said term at the end of the first three years thereof if the said Susan Potter her executors administrators or authorized assigns shall give six months previous notice in writing to the said John William Everett his heirs or assigns of her or their desire in that behalf And also a proviso for suspension of the said rent or a fair proportion thereof in case of accidental fire from six months next after the happening thereof until the premises shall be restored The said lease shall contain covenants on the part of the said John William Everett his heirs or assigns that the said Susan Potter her executors administrators and authorized assigns may on due payment by her and them of the said yearly rent to be reserved as aforesaid and on the performance and observance of the covenants by the lessee in the said lease to be contained quietly enjoy the premises to be demised without eviction or disturbance by the said John William Everett his heirs or assigns or any person claiming through or in trust for him or them And that he the said John William Everett his heirs or assigns will during the continuance of the said term keep the outside of the said premises in good and sufficient condition and repair   The said Susan Potter her executors administrators or authorized assigns shall duly execute and deliver to the said John William Everett his heirs or assigns a counterpart of the said lease   The said lease and counterpart shall be prepared by the Solicitor of the said John William Everett his heirs or assigns and the expenses of preparing and executing this agreement and the said lease and counterpart and all other incidental expenses shall be paid by the said Susan Potter her executors administrators or authorized assigns Until the execution of the said lease or the expiration or other sooner determination of the said term whichever shall first happen the said premises shall be held by the said Susan Potter her executors administrators or authorized assigns at the rent aforesaid and subject to the covenants and conditions to be contained in the said lease as aforesaid so far as the rules of law will permit.   IN WITNESS whereof the said parties to these presents have hereunto set their hands the day and year first above written.

JOHN WILLIAM EVERETT.

Signature to this agreement.
G. E. BROWN.

Form of Ordinary Receipt.

LONDON, May 2nd, 18—.

Received of Mr. John Frost, Twenty-nine pounds, twelve shillings and sixpence.

£29 12s. 6d. C. CUTHBERT.

N.B.—All receipts for sums of Two pounds and upwards require to have a receipt stamp affixed to them, which stamp should be cancelled by being written across. The penalty for evading this law is £10 under £100, £20 above that sum.

Form of Receipt for Rent.

LONDON, *August 18th, 18—.*

Received of A. Wigram, Esq., Fifteen pounds, being one quarter's rent due on Midsummer Day last, for the premises occupied by him at No. 14, South Rupert Street, W.C.

£15 0s. 0d.   T. PHILLIPS.

Form of Notice to Quit, from Landlord to Tenant.

MADAM,

I hereby give you notice to quit the house and appurtenances, situate at 17, Gloucester Road, which you now hold of me, on or before 25th of December next.

Dated 23rd of June, 1883.

Signed   JOHN WILLIAM EVERETT (Landlord).

To MISS POTTER.

Form of Notice to Quit, from a Tenant to a Landlord.

SIR,

I hereby give you notice that on or before the 25th of December next, I shall quit and deliver up possession of the house and premises I now hold of you, situate at 17, Gloucester Road, in the parish of St. Peter's, in the county of Middlesex.

Dated this 23rd day of June, 1883.

Witness, M. PRYKE.   SUSAN POTTER.

To MR. EVERETT.

Form of Cheque to " Bearer."

LONDON, *Dec.* 8th, 18—.

To the London Joint-Stock Bank,
    Chancery Lane Branch.

Pay to ——— or bearer, One Hundred pounds.

T. ROBINSON.

£100.

o

Form of Cheque to "Order."

LONDON, *Dec. 8th*, 18—.

To the London Joint-Stock Bank,
  Chancery Lane Branch.

Pay to —— or order, One Hundred pounds.

T. ROBINSON.

£100.

This form will require, previous to payment, the endorsement of the party to whom it is made payable.

Form of a Promissory Note.

LONDON, *July 1st*, 18—

£100.

Three Months after date, I promise to pay to Mr. Henry Jones, or order, One Hundred pounds, for value received.

T. ROBINSON.

Payable at ——

To make this a negotiable document it has to be endorsed by being signed across the back, by the party to whom it is made payable.

Form of an Ordinary Bill of Exchange.

LONDON, *May 1st*, 18—.

£100.

Three Months after date, pay to me or my order One Hundred pounds.   Value received.

T. ROBINSON.

To MR. HENRY JONES, LIVERPOOL.

To make this a negotiable document it has to be accepted by being signed across the face, by the party on whom it is drawn, and endorsed on the back by the drawer.

This admits of the following change, according to circumstances : instead of "three months after date," it may be "at sight," or at such a time "after sight," or at such a specified time, or "on demand ; " and the instruction to pay may be "to A. B. or order."

Form of a Foreign Bill of Exchange.

PARIS, *June 1st,* 18—.

£100.

Sixty days after sight of this First of Exchange (Second and Third unpaid) pay to the order of Messrs. Jones and Robinson, One Hundred pounds sterling, value received; and charge to account, with or without advice of

WILLIAM SMITH.

To MR. THOMAS KELLY, MANCHESTER.

Payable in London.

The naming of the payee admits of the same variations as are exhibited in an ordinary Bill of Exchange. The time of payment may be, in like manner, variously expressed. The term "usance" is sometimes employed to express the period of running in foreign bills. It means a certain time fixed by custom as between any two places, and the period covered by a usance will therefore depend on the places of drawing and payment.

Form of Bill of Sale.

Know all men by these presents, that I, A. B., of ——, for and in consideration of the sum of ——, in hand, paid, at and before the sealing and delivery hereof, by C. D., of ——, the receipt whereof I do hereby acknowledge, have bargained and sold, and by these presents do bargain and sell, unto the said C. D., all the goods, household stuff, and implements of household, and all other goods whatsoever, mentioned in the schedule hereunto annexed, now remaining and being in ——. To have and to hold all and singular the goods, household stuff, and implements of household, and every of them, by these presents bargained and sold unto the said C. D., his executors, administrators, and assigns for ever. And I, the said A. B., for myself, my executors, and administrators, all and singular of the said goods unto the said C. D., his executors and administrators and assigns, and against all and every other person and persons whatsoever, shall and will warrant, and for ever defend by these presents; of which goods I, the said A. B., have put the said C. D. in possession by delivering him one silver candelabrum, &c., on the sealing hereof. In witness whereof, I have hereunto put my hand and seal, this —— day of ——, in the year of our Lord one thousand eight hundred and ——.

A. B.

Signed, sealed, and delivered, } C. D.
   in the presence of us   } E. F.

Form of Bill of Lading.

Shipped in good order and well-conditioned by Edward Irving & Co., in and upon the good ship called the *Victoria*, whereof is master for the present voyage Henry Steele, and now riding in the river Douro, and bound for London, fourteen hogsheads of red Port Wine, being marked and numbered as in the margin, and are to be delivered in the like good order and well-conditioned, at the aforesaid Port of London, the dangers of the seas only excepted, unto Mr. Thomas Jackson, or to his assigns, he or they paying freight for the said goods, fifty shillings sterling per ton, with primage and average accustomed. In witness whereof, the master of the said ship hath affirmed to three bills of lading, all of this tenor and date, one of which bills being accomplished the others to stand void.

HENRY STEELE

OPORTO, *October 9th*, 18—.

This form varies according to the goods conveyed, being a steam ship or sailing vessel.

(In the margin: a diamond shape containing "T. J", with "E. I. & Co." below it.)

Form of Will.

This is the last Will and Testament of Robert Parker, of 17, Church Road, Saffron Walden. I hereby give and devise to my wife, Jane Parker, her heirs, executors, and administrators, for her and their own use and benefit, absolutely and for ever, all my estate and effects, both real and personal, whatsoever and wheresoever, and of what nature and quality soever, and I hereby appoint her, the said Jane Parker, sole executrix of this my Will.

In witness whereof I have hereunto set my hand, this 1st day of June, one thousand eight hundred and eighty-three.

ROBERT PARKER.

Signed by the said Robert Parker in our presence, who in his presence and in the presence of each other at the same time, subscribe our names as witnesses hereto.

RICHARD REYNOLDS.
JAMES TURNER.

Residing at Saffron Walden.

FRENCH, LATIN, AND ITALIAN WORDS,

FREQUENTLY IN USE IN LETTER WRITING.

contretemps
esprit de corps
dramatis personæ
fidus Achates
alter ego
entente cordiale
rencontre
fait accompli
dénouement
coup de grâce
au revoir
fiasco
enfant gâté
parvenu
couleur de rose
régime
nolens volens
major-domo
protégé
congé
de trop
carte blanche
sine quâ non
minus
douceur
gratis
quid pro quo
entre nous
embarras do richesses
furore

gusto
empressement
verve
piquant
con amore
sang froid
nonchalance
insouciance
bouleverser
qui vive
éperdu
tête montée
esclandre
triste
ennui
fête champêtre
connoisseur
dilettante
comme il faut
savoir faire
savoir vivre
distingué
bizarre
outré
mauvaise honte
bête noire
prestige
amour propre
coup d'œil
sans cérémonie

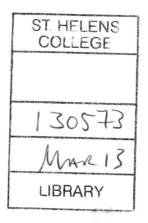
Lightning Source UK Ltd.
Milton Keynes UK
UKOW051110190213

206497UK00001B/117/P